The Carnegie-Mellon Curriculum
for Undergraduate Computer Science

The Carnegie-Mellon Curriculum for Undergraduate Computer Science

Edited by
Mary Shaw

This curriculum and its description were developed during the period 1981–1984 by Stephen D. Brookes, Marc Donner, James Driscoll, Michael Mauldin, Randy Pausch, William L. Scherlis, Mary Shaw, and Alfred Z. Spector

Springer-Verlag
New York Berlin Heidelberg Tokyo

Mary Shaw
Stephen D. Brookes
Marc Donner
James Driscoll

Michael Mauldin
Randy Pausch
William L. Scherlis
Alfred Z. Spector

Computer Science Department
Carnegie-Mellon University
Pittsburgh, Pennsylvania 15213
U.S.A.

(C.R.) Computer Classification: K.3

Chapter 7 is reprinted from M. Shaw and A. Ralston, "Curriculum'78—Is Computer Science Really That Unmathematical?," *Communication of the ACM*, February, 1980. Copyright 1980, Association for Computing Machinery, Inc., reprinted by permission.

Library of Congress Cataloging in Publication Data
Main entry under title:
The Carnegie-Mellon curriculum for undergraduate computer
    science.
    "This curriculum and its description were developed
during the period 1981–1984 by Stephen D. Brookes. . .
et al."
    Bibliography: p.
    Includes index.
    1. Computers–Study and teaching. 2. Carnegie-Mellon
University. I. Shaw, Mary
QA76.27.C37   1984   001.64'07'11   84-23468

With 5 Illustrations

9 8 7 6 5 4 3 2 1

ISBN-13: 978-0-387-96099-9   e-ISBN-13: 978-1-4612-5080-7
DOI: 10.1007/978-1-4612-5080-7

Preface

Carnegie-Mellon has had a Computer Science Department and a PhD degree program since 1965, but an undergraduate major leading to a Bachelor's degree in Computer Science has never been offered. Nevertheless, a set of undergraduate courses is taught, and the Mathematics Department offers an option that relies heavily on these courses. Thus, an undergraduate student who wishes to study computer science will usually take a mathematics degree with a computer science option.

On a number of occasions over the past decade, the Computer Science Department has considered offering an undergraduate Computer Science major. Until recently, the decision has always been negative. In the Spring of 1981, however, the Department agreed to consider taking steps toward offering a major. A Curriculum Design Group was formed to identify the curriculum that would support a major. This group included Stephen D. Brookes, Marc Donner, James Driscoll, Michael Mauldin, Randy Pausch, William L. Scherlis, Mary Shaw, and Alfred Z. Spector. This book presents the result of the group's efforts.

We decided that the first step should be a thorough review of the existing curriculum. The content of the present courses has evolved through the years, and a complete review has not been done in quite some time. Because computer science is evolving rapidly, we felt that the changing nature of computers and computing was not adequately reflected by the existing curriculum. As a result, we decided to reconsider the entire curriculum, including both computer science courses and courses that will probably be offered by other departments. Our goals are described in a technical report [104] (reprinted in [103]) and briefly reviewed in Chapter 4.

At the same time as this design was underway, Carnegie-Mellon was developing a university-wide personal computer network. There was no substantial interaction between the curriculum design and the campus network project that was being designed concurrently, but we tried to identify ways to take advantage of advanced computing technology as we developed courses. In general, however, we believe that Computer Science Departments should coordinate their plans with those of their universities, which have a growing need to use computers in support of undergraduate education and to develop courses that deal with computation in fields other than computer science. We hope that by systematically including software support requirements in course designs we can influence the development of university computing facilities and justify software development as an ordinary part of course development.

Acknowledgments

A curriculum necessarily spans its discipline; its designers need all the help they can get. We have received a great deal. Though it is impossible to acknowledge all of it, we want to express our appreciation to some of the people who have affected our thinking most significantly. Thanks, then:

- ▸ To the Carnegie-Mellon Computer Science Department for support and encouragement in this project.

- ▸ To the following people, who contributed significantly to the design of individual courses: Jon Bentley, Ellen Borison, Jaime Carbonell, Wes Clark, Carl Ebeling, Allan Fisher, Ed Frank, Geoff Hinton, Takeo Kanade, Elaine Kant, Monica Lam, Dan Leivant, Matt Mason, Dana Scott, John Shen, Chris Stephenson, Hank Walker, Bob Wedig, and Bill Wulf.

- ▸ To Jill Fain, Cynthia Hibbard, Allen Newell, and Steve Shafer, who provided extensive critical comments on drafts of the proposal.

- ▸ To previous members of this project team, Jon Bentley and Guy Steele. Their participation in the early stages of the design contributed enormously to the final philosophy and structure.

- ▸ To members of the IEEE/ACM Software Engineering Planning Group. Section 2.2 was prepared while its author was working on both reports, and many of the ideas were developed or refined during the discussions at the planning meeting in September 1982.

- ▸ To the participants of the Sloan Conference/Workshop on the first two years of College Mathematics, from which the first version of our discrete mathematics syllabus emerged.

- ▸ To Roy Ogawa and Dana Scott for helpful comments on the original manuscript of chapter 8.

- ▸ To Betsy Grgurich, who typed, edited, and reformatted many, many versions of the manuscript.

Table of Contents

1. Introduction and Overview

The Carnegie-Mellon Computer Science Department's Curriculum Design Project examined the current state of computer science and computer science curricula, projected the requirements for undergraduate education in computer science over the next decade, and developed a curriculum suitable for a computer science major. This book presents the resulting design.

For many years Carnegie-Mellon has had a computer science curriculum (a body of courses), but it has never had a computer science major (a formal degree program). The department has adopted the curriculum presented here as a basis for major reorganization of its undergraduate offerings, though resource limitations will probably prevent a complete implementation of the curriculum. Some reasonable subset of the curriculum could form the basis for a computer science major. However, a curriculum is a necessary but not a sufficient condition for a major and the other issues, such as resource requirements, are not addressed here.

1.1. Goals of the Curriculum Design

Computer science is opening new specialties in many fields, and as a result the pattern of student involvement in university computing is changing. During the next decade, four different undergraduate populations within the university will require distinct kinds of education about computer science. These groups are:

► The *computer scientists*, students actually majoring in computer science,

► The *computing specialists*, students in computational specializations within other disciplines,

► The *occasional programmers*, students who will write programs for personal use; and

► The *casual users*, students who will make only casual use of computers.

In this design project we took as our goal the design of a curriculum for the first group of students: those interested primarily in computer science. We have formulated a unified view of the discipline, identified a suitable collection of courses, and defined the content requirement for a major. We chose not to consider the university resources required to support such a curriculum.

In this design, we did not address the computer science education of non-majors, but universities should do so. This report discusses the needs of these students and some suitable responses, but it does not go into depth. New curriculum designs will be required for the computer specialists and the casual users.

1.2. Educational Philosophy

We set out to develop a curriculum that would support a computer science degree of the highest quality. Such a curriculum requires a balanced blend of fundamental conceptual material and examples drawn from the best of current practice. In many ways, our educational philosophy is based directly on the Carnegie Plan for education [21, 22, 32, 88], which emphasizes an integrated understanding of basic concepts and the application of those concepts to practical problems. We believe that a curriculum with a small common core and a broad selection of advanced courses supports a variety of computer science specializations including both terminal and nonterminal programs.

1.3. Character of the Curriculum

We have designed a computer science curriculum consistent with this educational philosophy. The curriculum includes a unified overview of computer science, the content requirements for a computer science major, and detailed descriptions of a number of computer science courses. The curriculum has interactions with offerings in other departments, but these relations are not completely specified.

The design recognizes that computer science is a maturing field with a growing set of increasingly comprehensive models and theories. As such, it relies very heavily on mathematics, and it has close ties to several other disciplines. Because the field is changing rapidly, students need fundamental knowledge that they can adapt to new situations. In addition, students must be able to apply their knowledge to real problems, and they must be able to generate tasteful and cost-effective solutions to these problems. In this curriculum, the integration of theory and practice is a theme of virtually every course.

We have sketched outlines for thirty computer science courses. They include seven courses in systems and design, three courses in programming languages, two courses in algorithms and analysis, three courses in computer hardware systems, one course in elementary discrete mathematics, four courses in theory and mathematical foundations, four courses in artificial intelligence, one course in graphics, and five independent study, project, or seminar courses. Many of these courses are completely new, and the rest are revised from the form in which they currently exist at Carnegie-Mellon. As a result, a major effort will be required to implement the individual course designs.

In addition to the courses we define here, we have identified a number of courses generally offered by other departments that present material relevant to computer science. Though such material is often conceptually part of a computer science education, we did not develop new descriptions for such courses.

We have also proposed requirements for a computer science major based on this curriculum. These requirements are the basis for a liberal professional education. The required core is small (five specific courses plus two courses constrained to specific areas), thereby allowing a variety of specializations within the major. Additional requirements assure breadth, both by requiring substantial exposure to humanities. social sciences, and fine arts and by requiring a concentration of study outside the major.

1.4. Innovations in the Curriculum

Because the design was carried out without prior commitment to course organizations, the resulting organization is based on the structure of modern computer science rather than on traditional course divisions. The major innovative characteristics of the resulting curriculum include the following:

- *Organization around a core.* The curriculum consists of a core of courses that present the basis of the field together with a set of more advanced courses that provide depth of knowledge. The core courses emphasize the mathematical foundations of the field in practical settings.
- *Curriculum integration.* The courses are carefully integrated with each other, and strong prerequisite relations ensure that the material will be presented in a coherent order. Subareas often have one course that provides a broad introduction and a sequence of courses that provide greater depth.
- *Courses designed around ideas rather than artifacts.* Topics based on common ideas often appear in a single course, even if the topics are not traditionally taught together. This often entails rearrangement of traditional course boundaries; it also allows integration of theory and practice.
- *Use of proper computer support.* Many courses require extensive access to computers and software to illustrate points being made in the course. Though the forthcoming campus-wide personal computer system at Carnegie-Mellon will aid in this, we have presented the functional requirements for computer support rather than discussing specific ways to use personal computers.

After developing a global view of the curriculum, we derived specific courses. We re-derived the need for an elementary sequence much like the one developed at Carnegie-Mellon in the late 1970's (211 and 212)[1] This provides a solid foundation for sequences of advanced courses. In many cases, the initial course of an advanced sequence is eminently suited for a

---

[1]Numbers in this section refer to course numbers. Syllabi for these courses appear in Chapter 11.

student who wants to use the techniques of an area without specializing in it. The major new courses and course sequences include

- ▶ A sophomore course that provides a concrete appreciation of the nature of computation through a unified view of hardware, software, and theory (240).
- ▶ A reorganization of the traditional operating systems course that integrates the hardware, software, and theoretical views of concurrency, generalizes the resource management aspect of operating systems, deals with complex, long-lived data and integrates hardware and software aspects of communication (310, 410, 411).
- ▶ A new course that presents module-level program organizations and software development techniques. This course fills a gap between the courses that teach data structures or program fragments and the courses that deal with constructing systems from modules (313).
- ▶ A reorganization of the traditional comparative programming languages and compiler construction courses. The resulting courses focus first on programming languages and user interfaces, progresses to the use of advanced software tools for system (especially compiler) development, and culminate in language design and compiler construction techniques (320, 420, 421).
- ▶ A set of courses that present algorithms and the mathematical foundations of computer science with emphasis on integrating the practical aspects of the material with the presentation of the theory. The courses cover algorithms, logic, formal languages, automata, computability, complexity, and theory of programming languages (330, 350, 351, 430, 450, 451).
- ▶ A set of artificial intelligence courses that establish parallel sequences for the cognitive processing and robotics aspects of AI (360,361,460,461).

In addition, we plan joint development of a course for advanced students that establishes a basis for responsible evaluation of the consequences of computing and for interpreting the technology to laymen (380).

1.5. Organization of the Book

The setting for this design is discussed in Chapter 2. Roles for the university to play in the education of both majors and non-majors are examined in Chapter 3. Our general educational philosophy is defined in more detail in Chapter 4. Chapter 5 presents our integrated view of the content of computer science. Chapter 6 shows how majors (Bachelor's degree programs) could be created from the courses of this curriculum. Chapters 7 and 8 reprint articles on the role of mathematics in computer science and the nature of the curriculum support that computer science needs from mathematics. Chapter 9 discusses the design of the basic course, FUNDAMENTAL STRUCTURES OF COMPUTER SCIENCE I AND II [211/212]. Chapter 10 discusses the rationale for our organization. Outlines for the computer science courses we propose are presented in Chapter 11. Chapter 12 lists courses from other departments that cover related material.

2. The Nature of Computer Science

We begin by surveying the field of computer science, projecting some future developments, and placing the field in context in academia and society. In Section 2.1, we describe the scope of the field we consider to be computer science. In Section 2.2 we make some projections about the kind of computing we may be doing ten years hence. On the basis of these projections, we predict some of the issues the field must face over the next decade and some of the changes we must anticipate.

2.1. Working Definition of Computer Science

There is no generally accepted definition of the field of computer science, and we do not expect to remedy that deficiency here. Nevertheless, we need a characterization of the discipline in order to focus our discussions. The curriculum design presented in this report is based on the following working definition.

Computer science is concerned with the study of computers and of the phenomena connected with computing, notably algorithms, programs, and programming. A major objective of the discipline is the formulation of a systematic body of knowledge, theories, and models to explain the properties of computers and of these related phenomena. Computer (or computational) systems often exhibit extremely complex structure and behavior; techniques for identifying, quantifying, and managing complexity are therefore central to computer science. The discipline is also concerned with producing solutions to technological (real-world) problems using a detailed knowledge of the properties and the applicability of current computing technology. Since there are usually many different ways to solve a problem, an important engineering activity is evaluating, comparing, and selecting alternatives on the basis of criteria such as cost or efficiency. Unlike the natural sciences, computer science studies objects and systems that are artificial. Since both the rules and the artifacts can be modified by the scientist, this can be both a problem and an advantage.

A description of computer science should include not only its subject matter, but also its characteristic paradigms and modes of analysis, reasoning, and problem solving. Computer science borrows heavily from mathematics, using analytic and synthetic techniques such as inductive definitions and case analysis. But it is not exclusively a formal, quantitative field, because the need for practical systems suitable for human use leads the field to rely, for example, on design and modelling techniques from engineering and on studies of human performance and behavior from psychology. In addition, the leading edge of computer science is moving rapidly. As a result, particular examples or techniques become obsolete and research results move rapidly into the body of pragmatic knowledge.

Using this working definition as a starting point, we conclude that the curriculum must deal with:

- ▶ Computers and related phenomena: machines and computations, both real and abstract.
- ▶ Algorithms, programs, and programming: techniques for creating and analyzing them.
- ▶ Complex structure and behavior of information: how to identify, quantify, and manage it.
- ▶ Engineering concerns: cost-effective solutions to technological problems and the application of current technology.
- ▶ Design tradeoffs: how to compare and select alternatives with respect to given criteria, and some appropriate criteria for such decisions.
- ▶ Human performance: the ways people use computers and the ways they manage complex problems.

Computer science is growing rapidly, and the curriculum must be able to react rapidly as well. It must be flexible enough to allow allow adaptation to changes in both technology and current philosophy, and it must provide students with an education of lasting value despite these changes. It must be broad enough to train computer scientists who can interpret the evolution of computer science to laymen. Further, it must make students aware of the roles of computers in society, because as professionals in a field that will so change society they must be able to make informed, responsible decisions that will affect the lives of many.

2.2. A View of Future Computing

The nature of computing, and hence of computer science, is changing rapidly. Many topics that now seem interesting will be obsolete or irrelevant within ten years. If the curriculum we design now is to remain effective into the 1990's, we must try to understand the forces that are shaping the field and to anticipate the roles that computing and computer science will play in the future. This section points out some of the trends that will affect the field over the next decade and describes some of the new phenomena and issues that may arise.

Computers are becoming smaller and cheaper, and they are being distributed across a wider and more varied population. Important current trends include:

- ▶ Decreasing hardware costs
- ▶ Increasing share of computing costs attributable to software
- ▶ Increasing expectations about the power and reliability of application systems
- ▶ Increasing range of applications, particularly those on which lives will depend

- Increasing development of distributed computing and convenient network access
- Increasing availability of computing power, especially in homes
- Widening view of computers as an information utility and a basis for electronic publishing
- Increasing quality of interfaces to humans (voice, high-performance graphics)
- Increasing exposure of naive people to computers, both at home and in the work place
- Increasing general reliance on computers for day-to-day operations.
- Continuing or increasing shortage of qualified professionals
- Continuing misunderstanding of the nature of software
- Increasing importance of "intelligent" systems

On the basis of these trends, we can extrapolate some future developments:

- *Pervasive Consumer Computing:* Computers will be extremely widespread, both as multiple-purpose machines in homes and offices and as dedicated machines for applications such as environment control and hazard monitoring. Most of the users of these machines will be naive—certainly the majority of them will not be programmers. As a result, most of the *users* of programs will not be *creators* of programs.

- *Information Utility:* We will come to think of computers primarily as tools for communicating and for accessing information, rather than primarily as calculating machines. Networks will provide a medium for making available numerous public databases, both passive (catalogs, library facilities, newspapers, bulletin boards) and active (newsletters, electronic mail individualized entertainment). Real-time control applications will become more prevalent.

- *Broad Range of Applications:* The range of applications will continue to broaden, and an increasing number will be applications in which unreliable computation could lead to risk of human life. As a result of this and of widespread use by nonprogrammers, much of the software will provide packaged services that require little, if any, programming. There will be substantial economic incentives for producing general systems that can be tuned to individual, possibly idiosyncratic, requirements.

- *Changes in the Workplace:* Distributed systems and networks will facilitate a distributed workplace, but we doubt that the norm for office workers will be to work at home instead of in an office. Electronic communication will speed communication, but computers will not replace human interaction for decision-making. Electronic work stations will change the nature of work that now depends on paper flow, and robotics will substantially change manufacturing.

▶ *Massively More Complex Computers:* Some computer networks and large computers will be replaced by or evolve into massive computer systems whose capacity is orders of magnitude greater than that of any system now available. These new systems may include enormous databases (nationwide banking records, interactive consumer catalogs, traffic information for ocean-going vessels, etc.), and be used by millions of people simultaneously. The first steps have already been taken by airline and hotel reservation systems.

▶ *Intelligent Systems:* Intelligent software systems will provide intellectual multipliers that substantially increase professional productivity in some areas. Intelligent robots will take over an increasing percentage of the industrial workload and perhaps even make a dent in the household chores. Increasingly sophisticated systems will lessen the need for programmers, and they may increase everyone's need for a basic understanding of computers. Further, today's expert systems may be tomorrow's oracles.

▶ *Effect on GNP:* The fraction of the GNP represented by computing and information handling—already large—will increase as our society becomes as dependent on information as on grain or metal.

Even if this projection is inaccurate in its details,there will nevertheless be a substantial qualitative shift in the role of computers in the world at large. The nature of education will surely be affected: we can already see the effects of pocket calculators on the teaching of elementary mathematics. Further, entertainment technology (e.g., Sesame Street and video games) has raised students' expectations about the educational process.

This view of the future raises a number of issues.

▶ *Consumer Concerns:* The use of computers by large numbers of nontechnical people, together with the increasing number of sensitive applications that involve computers, will raise issues about the responsibilities of vendors towards their products. These will certainly include analogs of the familiar problems associated with product and professional liability, merchantability and warrantability (guarantees), usability and reliability, licensing, copyrights, and product safety (e.g., development of an analog to the certification that Underwriters Laboratories provides for electrical products). Other problems, such as security and privacy concerns, will undoubtedly arise from the special nature of computers.

▶ *Production and Distribution:* An expanding role for computers and computer-related products and services in the retail marketplace will introduce new problems in manufacturing, sales and service, equitable methods of charging for shared resources, and industry compatibility standards. Another class of problems will center on how to create software for a mass market, perhaps including some notion of mass production of software (e.g., by tailoring packages rather than by writing code and by using software to construct software).

▶ *Safety and Security:* In addition to the consumer-safety issues, we can expect questions concerning licensing, product and professional liability, and the trustworthiness or integrity of data provided via public databases. Existing concerns about security and privacy will increase. These concerns will be particularly acute where human life is at stake.

▶ *Economic Impact:* The economic impact of these major innovations will be widespread. Of particular concern for the computing industry will be the interplay between technological development and limiting factors, such as productivity, on the growth of the information sector. Accurate software cost estimates and well-considered marketing policies will be vital as the computer industry matures. Some of the most important economic changes will involve personnel, especially when unskilled positions are eliminated through automation or replaced by jobs requiring a high level of technical expertise.

▶ *Human Issues:* Currently, people deal directly with computers primarily by choice. As computers become pervasive, people will interact with them through necessity. There will be a variety of sociological consequences, including the necessity of systems designed for naive users, personnel dislocation caused by technical change, and major shifts in the content and style of education.

▶ *Social Issues:* The computer age could bring about a new underprivileged class of the computer illiterate. Women and minorities might make up the majority of this new class because of insufficient technical education. To prevent this situation computer scientists must be aware of the social implications of their work, and the society must be aware of the implications this new technology holds.

In response to these issues, universities must broaden the scope of their computer-related offerings in order to prepare students to use the new electronic tools and to adapt these tools to a variety of new uses. We believe that this is best accomplished by teaching students the principles that support current tools; current practices will rapidly become obsolete, and students must be prepared to adapt.

Our view of the future of computing cannot be entirely correct. To assure responsiveness, to unexpected developments, this curriculum is designed around fundamental concepts, such as control, data, system, and language, that are likely to remain central, rather than around traditional systems such as compilers and operating systems. Thus if in the next ten years, text editors replace compilers as prime examples in computer science courses, the new notions can be added in those courses which present the basic concepts necessary for writing text editors. These courses could use text editing as a practical example of these ideas, since each course presents both theory and practice. This approach maintains the consistency of the whole curriculum, and retains the old prerequisite structure, and is thus far superior to merely adding a new "text editor" course.

In some cases, we attempt to foresee future developments; where this is the case, the implementation notes at the end of each course description indicate how the course may be changed to handle new ideas and requirements. An example of this is DISCRETE MATHEMATICS [150], which may soon be expanded into two courses. Another example is VLSI SYSTEMS [441]; VLSI design is a composite of many fundamental ideas which might be taught in other courses on circuit and algorithm design. As the field matures, material from the VLSI course is likely to be incorporated in more basic courses.

3. Roles for Universities

Computer science has grown rapidly throughout its short lifetime. Universities have been major contributors to that growth, and they bear a major responsibility for dissemination of knowledge about computer science. Professional education in computer science is growing more rigorous, and we expect an increasing need for students to master a growing set of fundamental concepts. Mere programming skill will no longer suffice for most computing professionals. The field will require solid technical expertise comparable to that expected of engineers, and most development work will require genuine competence in both the application field and computer science. In addition, many people will need to use computers in sophisticated ways and understand the implications of the spreading computer technology. Universities must begin now to respond to these emerging needs.

The widespread availability of inexpensive computation will also affect the process of education. Applications will range from direct implementation of routine exercises to innovative systems that present material in fundamentally different ways from conventional courses. Courses that make extensive use of computation will take on the character of laboratory courses; the development of computer support, especially of programs suitable for student use, will be at least as difficult as development of new textbooks.

This chapter discusses roles for computing in universities. It begins with an analysis of the audiences for computer science education—the groups of students who need some kind of computer science education. Next, it describes the potential for exploiting computing technology in the educational process. Finally, it assesses the current state of affairs in the computer science curriculum establishment and argues that existing curriculum designs are not adequate.

3.1. The Audience

Because of the growing importance of computers in many fields, universities now have a responsibility for teaching several distinct groups of students about computers and about computer science. In this section, we examine the pattern of student involvement with computing and suggest that a significant change in that pattern is taking place. We describe several distinct groups of students and discuss the kind of computer science education each group needs. We identify one group, the computer science majors, as the focus of this report, and we recommend that curriculum design efforts be undertaken for two other groups.

In the early 1970's many technical students and a few nontechnical students took some kind of introductory programming course. Perhaps half of these students went on to take a few more computer science courses; these courses usually emphasized programming languages or programming techniques. Only a few students pursued computer science to the depth required of a major.

This pattern of student involvement in computing can be illustrated by the histogram of Figure 3-1(a), whose vertical axis represents increased technical depth in computing and whose horizontal axis represents the fraction of the student body involved. In this figure we see three groups: a modest number of computer science majors, a significant number of students with extensive programming experience and some exposure to the ideas of computer science, and a large number of students with enough programming ability to use computers in their own work. It is important to note that most introductory courses and many of the more advanced courses emphasized computer programming. As a result during the 1970's, the conceptual basis of computer science and the potential of computers for personal information processing were often slighted.

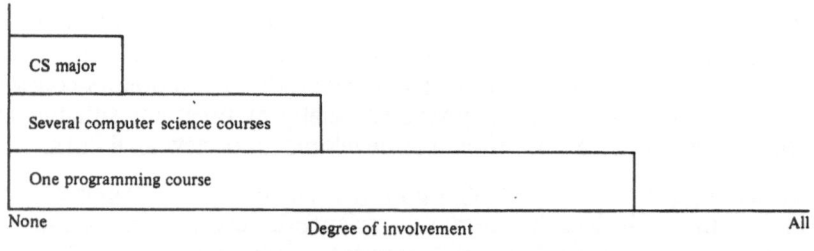

(a) Conventional pattern in the 1970's

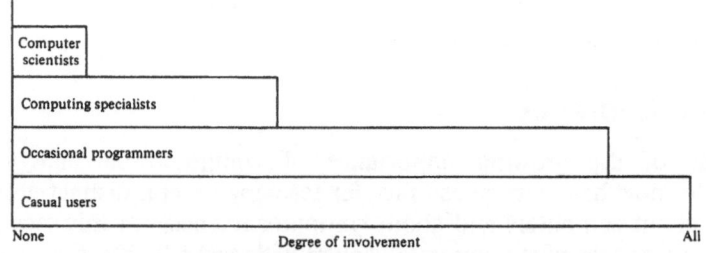

(b) Cross-disciplinary pattern expected in the 1980's

Figure 3-1:   Student Involvement with Computing in the 1970's and 1980's

Students graduating in the 1970's with degrees in computer science or with degrees in other disciplines coupled with some computing experience were often employed as programmers. Usually, it was expected that the students would grow into increasingly responsible technical or managerial positions. In most cases their professional growth either lay within computer science or involved an explicit shift to, for example, management.

In the 1980s, as computing becomes part of general competence and computer science moves from a narrow specialty to a component of the basic education of every student, this pattern will surely change. There is currently a documented shortage of computer professionals at all levels, from technicians to researchers [85]; this manpower shortage is projected to continue through the 1980s. We believe that a major component of the demand for bachelor's and master's level computer professionals will soon be for computer specialists—students with advanced technical competence in computing as an integral component of computing specializations within other disciplines. Such joint education in computer science and another discipline is now seriously neglected; indeed, many of the students who currently select computer science majors might be better served by computing specializations in other departments. In addition, the criteria for general literacy in the university at large will require education for large numbers of casual users—students who will *use* a variety of sophisticated programs and packages but who will do very little *creation* of programs.

From these predictions and the sketch of future trends in Section 2.2 we can project a very different profile for student involvement in computing in the 1980's than the one we saw in the 1970's. Figure 3-1(b) shows the pattern of student computing experience that we expect to see in this decade. We expect, as before, a modest number of computer science majors. These should be students planning on graduate work in computer science or students who want to work directly within the computer industry. We project the number of computer science majors to be smaller than the demand currently seen in many schools because we expect much of that demand to be redirected to the second group—joint majors who master the fundamentals of both computer science and another discipline, then specialize in a computational branch of the other discipline. A third group of students—occasional programmers—may need opportunities (e.g., short introductions to the use of special packages or particular languages) that are not properly provided within an academic department. Finally, we expect that virtually all students will need an introduction to the use of computers and the role of computers in modern society.

The primary objective of this project has been to design a curriculum for computer science majors. We believe that a single curriculum can suffice for both terminal and nonterminal students. Modern computer science requires a core of fundamental material for both groups of students, and a program with flexibility in the use of electives can be tailored to a variety of individual needs.

We also see a need for intermediate-to-advanced computer science training for students who will become computing specialists within some discipline other than computer science. Professional specialization of this sort requires genuine competence in both fields—unlike present applications programming. We see a need for joint majors with closer cooperation between departments than is usually implied by a double major. Such joint programs might include scientific computation (in cooperation with a mathematics or physics department), human-computer interaction (with a psychology department), music synthesis and composers' tools (with a music department), computer-aided design (with a design or architecture department), or information systems (with an economics or management department). Students pursuing these joint majors should take at least the fundamental courses in computer science, the fundamental courses in a second discipline, and additional courses that deal with computing specialization within the second discipline.

Many students will want to use computers in personal projects. This will often involve writing programs. These students can be served by the same basic and elementary courses as students who will become more deeply involved in computer science. In addition, there will be a need for education about certain computing topics that do not fall within a computer science curriculum. Many of these topics are so narrowly directed at specific programs or programming languages that it is not appropriate for them to carry academic credit; for such topics, a program of tutorials in a nonacademic arm of the university should be considered.

An educational program must also be developed for students who will make only casual personal use of computing. The major need is for a fundamentally new introductory course. This course should introduce the nature of computing, show the social implications of widespread computing, make students comfortable accessing an information utility, and develop fluency in the use of packaged software. It should not be a programming course as such, though it should provide some elementary programming experience. This course could also provide an opportunity to introduce nontechnical students to problem solving, deductive reasoning, and analytic thinking in a setting where they could get direct experience and immediate feedback.

We conclude that there are four significant roles for universities to play in computer-related education. These include

- Educating future computer scientists at all degree levels—the *computer scientists,*
- Educating students who are computer scientists but who will bring computing expertise to their own fields of specialization—the *computing specialists,*
- Educating people who need modest programming skills—the *occasional programmers,* and
- Educating the entire university population, especially the *casual users,* about the potential and use of computers.

This curriculum design addresses only the first group: the computer science majors. We recommend that separate studies be undertaken to study computational specializations in other disciplines and computing education for the university population as a whole. We do not see a major problem with educating students who need only modest programming skills.

3.2. Use of Computing Technology in Education

In addition to organizing the content of computer science, a modern curriculum design must consider ways to use computing technology in the educational process. It is no longer unusual to rely on computers for course support; applications range from ordinary bookkeeping for course administration through novel interactive teaching systems. It is important, however, to avoid confusing education about the substance of computer science with the use of computers in education. In this section, we are primarily concerned with the use of computers in computer science education. We consider both the use of computers in the general educational process and the specific needs of computer science courses to use computing facilities as course laboratories.

At Carnegie-Mellon and a number of other institutions, computer resources are already commonly used for many of the mundane activities that are part of every course. These include distributing information to students; electronic mail between students, instructors, and teaching assistants; electronic collection of assignments; text processing; and record keeping. Further progress in this area requires a substantial commitment to application software development. The design of this software must address not only the function of the software but also the way it will be used, since the interface to the users is what makes the computer a worthwhile tool in this area. At Carnegie-Mellon, the University Center for Design of Educational Computing provides a centralized base for innovative uses of computers in education.

At Carnegie-Mellon, computer support for the students in the courses dates back at least to the 1950's, when the Graduate School of Industrial Administration (GSIA) introduced the "Management Game" (a computer-based management simulation of a detergent industry in which student teams competed for simulated profits). This course (much updated) is still required for second-year Master's students in GSIA. Other current computer-based instruction at Carnegie-Mellon includes microprocessor support for Physics laboratory courses, advanced graphics support for fluid mechanics, color graphics tools for art students, instructional programs for elementary concepts for formal logic, and a database of the French Revolution used in a freshman history course. In addition, plans are being made for an advanced computerized engineering laboratory in the engineering college, addition of animation and three-dimensional graphics in the art program, a Computer Music Center for computer-assisted composition and music analysis, and incorporation of computer support in a campus-wide writing program.

Applications such as these are becoming more common in computer science as well. At Carnegie-Mellon, interest dates back at least to a proposal for a software laboratory supported by interchangeable modules [23]. More recent activity in computer science includes simulators for abstract machines such as finite-state automata or Turing Machines and difficult-to-understand algorithms (e.g., van Dam's work at Brown [18]); program development environments (e.g., Teitelbaum's program synthesizer [112] at Cornell or Miller's Gnome [39], an adaptation of Gandalf, at Carnegie-Mellon). We can envision other automated tools and libraries of programs to read, modify, or use as elements of assignments.

There are many more opportunities for imaginative uses here, and we anticipate a steady increase in the demand for innovative "courseware." The more speculative ones include the transfer of research systems to the classroom, including expert systems, theorem-provers, transformation systems, and intelligent advice-givers with user models and tracking of student performance. We believe that some of the best opportunities for incorporating software in courses involve providing students with the software tools used by professionals (or possibly with scaled down versions of such tools). Some of the course-specific uses of computing technology for educational purposes are indicated in the individual descriptions of courses in Chapter 11.

In computer science, computers are not only pedagogical tools, they are the subject matter of many of the courses. Thus, computer science is an experimental science; computer science courses need undergraduate laboratories, just as physics, chemistry, and biology courses do. Unlike those disciplines; however, computer science laboratories for several courses can often share the physical facilities—the costs of establishing and maintaining the laboratories will be largely software and personnel costs. Undergraduate computer science courses require software support for the same reasons that more traditional laboratories require construction, maintenance, staffing, and supplies.

3.3. The ACM and IEEE Curricula

A variety of recommendations on undergraduate curriculua have been made by the ACM [1, 3] and the IEEE [54, 55]. None of these provides a suitable foundation for a curriculum that meets the needs described above.

The major shortcoming of the ACM and IEEE designs is that they seem to be merely summaries of existing curricula rather than projections designed to last for the next decade. We believe, however, that a curriculum design should provide leadership for the curriculum plans of individual schools. Any actual implementation will involve compromise and dilution, so a design should provide a level of aspiration and a direction of development rather than simply an inventory of current practice.

There are two chief reasons why we did not simply develop a curriculum directly based on the ACM recommendation. First, the ACM proposal is based more on the status quo in computer education than on any attempt to unify the intellectual content of computer science.   Second, the ACM curriculum relegates mathematics to a totally inadequate position—an attitude perhaps appropriate for a data processing curriculum, but not for a computer science curriculum.

The IEEE computer engineering curriculum [54] is also disappointing, even in its revised form as a "model program" [55]. Its balance of hardware, software, and theory is heavily biased toward hardware, and it fails to expose the important common fundamentals joining hardware and software. This might be reasonable for a curriculum directed purely at the electrical engineering side of the discipline, but the designers claim that the curriculum is suitable for computer science.

In addition to these well-known curriculum designs, we are beginning to see proposals about "software engineering" undergraduate programs as distinct from "computer science" programs. While many undergraduate programs are currently centered on the activity of programming, we believe that software engineering is a subset of what a well-trained computer scientist should know, and we believe that software engineering alone is too narrow a program for an undergraduate degree.

4. Objectives for the Curriculum

The curriculum described here was developed in response to objectives set forth in Spring 1982 [104]. The premises and goals from that project plan are reproduced in this section. Although these objectives were formulated with Carnegie-Mellon in mind, they are appropriate for a wide variety of institutions.

4.1. Premises

Certain assumptions about computer science, about education, and about CMU underlie this effort. It will be helpful to make them explicit:

- ▶ The major substance of an undergraduate computer science curriculum (as for any subject) should be fundamental conceptual material that transcends current technology and serves as a basis for future growth as well as for understanding current practice. This fundamental material should be reinforced by abundant examples drawn from the best of current practice.

- ▶ The CMU Computer Science Department should invest energy in a degree program only if that program is of very high quality—ranking among the top programs in the country.

- ▶ Whether or not the CMU Computer Science Department offers an undergraduate degree, a complete review of the undergraduate curriculum is in order.

- ▶ An undergraduate computer science curriculum design should address the entire curriculum, not just the courses offered by the Computer Science Department proper or even just the technical courses related to computer science.

We take as a working hypothesis the proposition that computer science is now mature enough—has enough intellectual substance —to warrant an undergraduate or master's-level curriculum and degree program. In this context, the curriculum design process can be thought of as an experiment to test that hypothesis.

4.2. Goals

Our specific objective is a high-quality computer science curriculum for CMU. This curriculum should also merit national recognition, both for the quality of the students it educates and as an exemplar for curricula at other schools.

Following the Carnegie Plan for education [21, 22, 32, 88], we want to design a curriculum through which a student can acquire:

- ▷ A thorough and integrated understanding of the fundamental conceptual material of computer science and the ability to apply this knowledge to the formulation and solution of real problems in computer science.

► A genuine competence in the orderly ways of thinking which scientists and engineers have always used in reaching sound, creative conclusions; with this competence, the student will be able to make decisions in higher professional work and as a citizen.

► An ability to learn independently with scholarly orderliness, so that after graduation the student will be able to grow in wisdom and keep abreast of the changing knowledge and problems of his or her profession and the society in which he or she lives.

► A philosophical outlook, breadth of knowledge, and sense of values which will increase the student's understanding and enjoyment of life and enable each student to recognize and deal effectively with the human, economic, and social aspects of his or her professional problems.

► An ability to communicate ideas to others.

The focus of the design will be on a liberal professional education with emphasis on problem-solving skills. Some of the words in the previous sentence are subject to various interpretations. "Liberal education" is broad, including humanities and social science courses plus technical courses outside the student's specialty. Liberal education includes communication skills, both for understanding the work of others and for communicating one's own work. Describing the education as "professional" recognizes the legitimate motivations of many students who value education because they can apply it rather than for pure intellectual enjoyment. "Problem-solving skills" refers to the ability to apply general concepts and methods from a variety of disciplines to all kinds of problems, abstract as well as practical, whose solutions require thought, insight, and creativity. Thus "problems" can range from the proof of a theorem to the design and construction of a specialized computer program and "skills" means creative intellectual ability, not merely the ability to perform repetitive routine actions.

5. The Content of Computer Science

This chapter surveys the content of computer science. The objectives are to present a coherent view of the conceptual structure of the field, to indicate the scope of our concerns, and to indicate connections with other fields. The discussion here is not constrained by the need to divide subject matter into courses; Chapter 11 shows how the material described here is organized into specific courses.

We realize that a unified discussion of ideas and concepts may not lead directly to a good organization for courses. That is, the conceptual structure provided here does not necessarily correspond to a pedagogical organization that forms a good foundation for a curriculum design. It is impossible, for example, to convey certain ideas without a background in the methods and conventions that support these ideas. Some issues (e.g., reliability, optimization, performance, adaptive design) appear in different forms and a variety of subject areas. Further, courses often focus on some kind of system (e.g., compilers or operating systems) in order to use a single rich example as a setting for a variety of related topics.

Computer science embraces a variety of ideas and modes of scientific thought that must be presented throughout a curriculum for their significance to be conveyed, even though they may appear as a single element of a conceptual organization. It is important for everyone who teaches the courses to present not only the concepts themselves but also an understanding of why these concepts are necessary for a wider understanding of the science. Because of the importance of these distributed ideas, we mention them explicitly here.

► *Abstraction and representation.* In a field such as computer science, in which the essential notions are quite abstract, it is important that certain patterns of reasoning be presented explicitly. Perhaps the most important of these is the management of complexity through abstraction and representation. Computer science deals with systems of human design that can appear to be extremely malleable, particularly when realized in software. This malleability belies the problem of handling complexity in such systems. The student must achieve a firm grasp of how abstraction is used to control complexity. In this style of reasoning, computer science bears a strong similarity to mathematics. Because mathematicians also deal with systems built upon human imagination, they have developed conceptual tools to manage complexity in the mathematical systems they create. Mathematical maturity and an understanding of how mathematics deals with complexity are essential for computer science students. Other important modes of thought for computer science are discussed later in this chapter.

▸ *Recurrent notions.* Certain particular ideas, such as naming and addressing, binding, state, resource management and allocation, and concurrency, recur in different contexts throughout computer science. It is important for them to be identified as recurrent ideas so students can consolidate their understanding. In our curriculum, there will usually be a single course charged with presenting an overview of a given idea in varied settings. This course should be sufficiently advanced that the student will have already encountered the topic in several forms; it should be elementary enough that many students will take it.

▸ *Theory and the practice of computing.* A good curriculum must be based on sound theories and models, and it must also teach these foundations in the context of good engineering practice. Most ideas in computer science can be presented in both theoretical and practical settings. These ideas are brought out most effectively when introduced at varying levels of abstraction. This is true not only because students frequently grasp ideas most easily in a concrete setting, but also because the varying range of presentations illustrates how abstract notions are realized in the concrete forms of programs or machines (or, conversely, how practical experience is expressed in abstract terms). It is for this reason that nearly all the courses in this curriculum make connections between theory and practice.

▸ *Cumulative experience with ideas.* Certain essential ideas must be developed over several courses for them to be completely assimilated. Students are exposed to the ideas early, but they may not be expected to articulate them or synthesize them until much later. For example, students first encounter data types when they learn to program. At this stage they are exposed to the idea, but they do not deal with it as a distinguishable concept. When the first programming language is re-examined in more depth, students perceive types as an identifiable programming concept. Later, students gain experience operating with types, for example by developing realizations for given type specifications. Only after this experience should students be expected to create new abstract type specifications. Since the development of such ideas must be distributed over several courses, it is necessary that each course instructor understand this progression.

The remainder of this chapter surveys the content of computer science, but without assigning topics to specific courses. The material is organized into four levels of sophistication in computer science.

5.1. Basics

This basic material provides fluency in the use of computers and familiarity with their capabilities that will be of interest to the broad population of students, not just to computer scientists. Within the next five to ten years, this material may well be regarded as an essential part of a good liberal education in any discipline. We expect that the skills that comprise fluency will change from programming skill (as at present) to a very different style of computer usage as the technology improves. The following basic material is expected to follow that change.

5.1.1. Content

Carnegie-Mellon, like many universities, is committed to requiring all students to use computers effectively. The introduction to computing for all these students should provide not merely the clerical skills required to use the computing resources, but also facility in logical and algorithmic thinking and an understanding of the notions of deductive reasoning, cause and effect, time and sequentiality, and state transition. This introduction should also provide students with an understanding of the role of computers in a technological society and of the responsibilities of a professional in the field.

These subjects constitute minimal literacy for a computer-based society:

▸ Basic computer literacy (i.e., as a naive user): understanding the capabilities of computers, dealing with an information utility (creating and using files), using existing programs and packages.

   The office/file cabinet model of computation
   Gaining access to simple useful facilities such as
      Computer mail*
      Simple files and campus databases (library card catalog, class schedules, etc.)
      Personal databases (calendars, resumes, etc.)
      Text formatting and writing tools (spelling checking, bibliographies, etc.)
   Using interactive programs and packages (editors, interactive spreadsheets, etc.)
      Non-textual interaction, drawing packages, painting and layout
   Networking and communications
      Using information services (bulletin boards, mailing lists, etc.)
      Using data facilities (central file servers, databases, etc.)
      The implications of information sharing

▸ Elementary facts about computers: organization, architecture (processors, primary and secondary memories, communication), concept of stored program.

   Processors and memory
   The fetch/execute cycle
   Storage devices (especially personal dismountable storage: disks, tapes, etc.)
   Representation of information with binary devices
      Binary numbers, encoding (e.g., character sets), instructions as data
   Networking, how information is shared between computers

- ▸ Elementary facts about programs: concept of algorithm, simple program structures, including control structures and procedures, declaration and use of data, use of libraries.

  Computation and sequential execution (following directions given in English
      or in a programming languages)
  Simple programming in a high level language
      Using and writing simple procedures
      Using integers, reals, strings, vectors, records
      File input and output

- ▸ Thinking about computers and programs: problem-solving ability, programming techniques, and concepts of correctness and performance.

  Elementary problem solving
  Mechanics and discipline of writing programs
      Simple program forms (filter on text file, summarization of data, etc.)
      Documentation
      Incremental coding strategy
      Debugging strategies, including data selection
  Correctness and the fact that programs can be reasoned about precisely
  Costs and the existence of time-space and efficiency-generality tradeoffs

- ▸ Role of computers in society: range of potential applications, appropriate and inappropriate use of computers.

  History of computers and their use
  View of computers as providing an information utility
  Potential future applications
  Social issues (computer crime, security and privacy, consumer issues, etc.)
  Ethics of computer use in an electronic community
  Careers in computers, technological displacement
  Impact of computers and robots on industry and employment
  Psychological and social aspects of computation
  Examples of applications

5.1.2. Skills

Skills developed in the basic curriculum include problem solving and simple deductive reasoning, the ability to carry on simple interactions with a computer such as using selected programs, and sufficient familiarity with computing to learn more as required.

5.2. Elementary Computer Science

These topics provide the foundation for a computer science degree; they are necessary but not sufficient. They are singled out here because they are relevant to all students seriously interested in computing, not only to computer scientists. Thus this material should be considered for joint programs with other disciplines.

Generally, this is material for sophomore and junior courses. Many of the topics are fundamental, forming the basis for development of more advanced material. The material described here also fosters functional fluency with contemporary systems. These skills are immediately useful; they provide experience in the use of the fundamental ideas, and the resulting experience makes richer examples accessible.

We organize the material into three rough categories, corresponding to the body of material itself, common modes of thought that students should be aware of, and skills associated with the material covered.

5.2.1. Content

This section outlines our view of the body of elementary computer science. It should be clear that some of these topics are drawn from other disciplines (such as mathematics and electrical engineering). Both theoretical and practical topics are included throughout the categories listed here.

▶ The nature of computation. Concept of algorithm; relation between algorithm and program. Elementary automata theory. (Supporting material from discrete mathematics.)

> Time, state, sequentiality, and concurrency
> Algorithms
> Abstract automata as model of computation
>> Finite-state automata
>> Additional power of Turing Machine
> Algorithms, programs that express them, and machines that execute them
> Probabilistic algorithms and heuristics
> Discrete mathematics:
>> Inductive definitions and proofs
>> Graphs, functions, relations
>> Propositional logic and proofs, set theory, boolean algebra
> Elementary notions of calculus and numerical analysis

▶ Computer organizations. The von Neumann model and machine/assembly language. Instruction-set-processor (ISP)-level and Processor-memory-switch (PMS)-level organizations, elementary network issues. At this level, the study is fairly superficial—the objective is understanding the structures in order to use them, rather than to be able to design new ones. (Supporting material from basic electrical engineering, including electricity, circuit design, and device characteristics.)

> Digital logic level
>> Basic digital concepts and terminology
>> Combinatorial circuits
>> Discrete time abstraction (clocks)
>> Circuit family abstraction
> Register transfer level
> Program level
>> Instruction formats and how they get interpreted

Concept of microcode
Architecture as specification of instruction set
Processor-Memory-Switch level
    Properties of processors
    Classes of switches (busses, crosspoints, etc.)
    Memory technology
        Characteristics of disks, tapes, drums, etc.
        Memory hierarchy
        Addressing techniques, data representation and register transfer
        Physical memory and addressing techniques
        Virtual memory and address mapping
    I/O and bus structures
Examples
    Calculators, microprocessors, and microcomputers
    Minicomputers and mainframe computers
    Multiprocessors, supercomputers

▶ **Program organizations.** Organization of simple programs and elementary modular composition. Data structures and some common program forms. Elementary concurrency issues. Informal reasoning about correctness and performance. The objective is design as well as use; at this level the rudimentary programming skills from the basic material are refined to a useful level.

Program development methods
    Structured programming
    Use of specification and verification
    Documentation
    Debugging and testing
Program organizations
    Data organization primitives (pointers, hashing, encoding, packing, etc.)
    Implementations of data types
    Abstract data types and their specification
    Some classical program organizations (filters, abstract data types,
        pattern-matching systems, table-driven interpreters, etc.)
    Imperative and applicative programming
    Recursion
    Matching data with control
Some classical algorithms
    Sorting and searching
    Numerical algorithms from linear algebra
    Graph algorithms

▶ **Languages and notations.** Programming languages. An appreciation of the power of good notation. Syntax and language description. Examples such as BNF and regular expressions. Recognition of the language component of any interface design and an awareness of the influence on design of pragmatic issues. (Supporting material from discrete mathematics.)

Language as communication, interface medium, means of shaping ideas
Syntax and semantics
Formal issues

Syntax: formal languages; regular and context-free languages; hierarchies of
    languages
Semantics:
    Denotational
    Operational
    Axiomatic (Hoare axioms or predicate transformers)
    Formal specification techniques: axioms and models
Classical programming language matters
    Organization of program control: iteration and recursion
    Functions, procedures, and exception handlers
    Data structures and declarations
    Scope, extent, and binding, including parameters
    Expression evaluation
    Abstraction facilities (procedures, types)
    Specification
Kinds of languages: applicative and procedural
Specialized languages
    Production systems
    Query languages
    Graphical interaction
    Semi-languages such as RPG, Visicalc, Makefile, editors
    Command languages

▶ **Design techniques.** Advanced programming and specification techniques. Also, relevant ideas from hardware design and other design disciplines.

Advanced programming techniques
Specification methods and languages
Decomposing programs into modules
Design tools
Documentation
Contemporary approaches to problem solving
Devising and evaluating alternatives
Evaluation criteria

▶ **Evaluation and analysis.** Analysis of algorithms, elementary models for performance. Criteria used for evaluation (correctness, speed, space, reliability, generality, complexity, etc.) and tradeoffs among them. (Supporting material from discrete mathematics.)

Correctness
    Specification and verification
Performance
    Formal models
    Bottleneck identification and elimination
Analysis of algorithms
Models and modelling
    What models are and how to use/construct them
    Empirical vs. analytic models
    Validation
    Specific models (at this level, introduction only)
        Queueing-theoretic models for operating systems and hardware
        Productivity and life-cycle models and their limitations
Human factors

► Advanced personal use of computers. Text manipulation, personal databases. Using an operating system (command files, Unix pipes, etc.). Graphical interaction. Access to libraries. Appreciation of what makes computers easy and hard to use. Reasonable and unreasonable social behavior; computing as a valuable commodity. (Supporting material from design and psychology.)

> Small examples of program development
> Practical matters:
>> Program segmentation and linkage
>> Linkers and loaders
>> Error recovery techniques
>> Systems and utility programs
> Text retrieval and processing (editing and document preparation)
> Introduction to operating systems concepts
> Batch, timesharing, and personal (dedicated) systems
> Elementary software engineering
>> Debugging, preventing debugging, test data selection
>> Organization of programming teams
>> Program organization for maintainability
>> Verification
>> Software libraries
> Ethics, privacy, implications of having a user community

► Some larger systems as examples. Study of systems large enough for complexity to become an issue. The objective is to generate some elementary familiarity with the systems and some of the issues, the hard problems of design and analysis come later.

> Compilers (relatively small complex system, but well-understood)
> Cognitive models (the human as a complex system)
> Databases (complexity of both size and interaction over time)
> Large software systems, such as operating systems (concurrency issues)
> Distributed systems

5.2.2. Modes of Thought

The following paradigms of computer science reasoning are illustrated in the topics listed above. Students will be better able to assimilate the technical material if they perceive the role of these paradigms.

► *Hypothesis and test.* That is, the classical scientific method. Models and their validation. Generalization as a technique for refining hypotheses.

► *Problem solving.* Finding and exploiting structure. Tradeoffs between generality and efficiency. Heuristic exploration of problem spaces.

► *Analysis and synthesis.* Managing complex systems by decomposition into parts. Development of systems on the basis of structural organization. Quantitative techniques.

► *Abstraction and realization.* Abstraction as control of complexity and detail. Realization as a process of binding underlying structure to implement an abstraction.

▶ *Inductive reasoning.* Drawing conclusions from limited observations.

5.2.3. Skills

Certain skills are useful and important for students to have when they deal with the ideas described above. These skills include simple programming skills such as coding and debugging, basic hardware logic design techniques, and the various mathematical skills related to discrete mathematics, such as inductive proofs and an ability to manipulate propositional calculus formulas.

5.3. Liberal Professional Education

These topics serve to make the computer scientist a well-rounded professional, able to appreciate the significance of work in other disciplines and able to apply computer science expertise to problems outside computer science.

This section also provides a taste of the interdependencies between computer science and other areas and suggests areas in which joint degrees might be appropriate.

5.3.1. General Scope

The curriculum for a liberal professional education must define the general coverage as well as the core material in the field of specialization. For us, that means a set of inclusive statements about the total scope and some more specific statements about areas that are related to computer science.

Note that a liberal professional education in other disciplines may require joint majors with or computing specializations in those fields. In this section we are dealing solely with the problem of a liberal professional education in computer science itself.

5.3.2. Liberal Education

We believe that students should be broadly educated. Our definition of a broad education includes mathematics, science, and engineering as well as humanities, social sciences, and the arts. A broad education is possibly more important in computer science than in other disciplines for two major reasons: First, computer science is strongly tied to many other disciplines, and as computers become more prevalent, the range of related disciplines can be expected to increase further. Second, there is an overwhelming need for computer scientists who are able to interpret the field to others.

5.3.3. Areas Related to Computer Science

The boundaries of computer science overlap with several other areas. Some of the material at the boundary should be developed (and possibly taught) with other departments. Specific offerings at the boundary should arise from close cooperation between the interested departments.

The following sections list topics where there is likely to be overlap between computer science and related fields. However, the list is by no means definitive. If curricula are established to help non-computer scientists specialize in computing aspects of their fields, it is likely that there would be many new courses that explore highly specific computing problems of various disciplines. Few such courses are included in this section.

5.3.3.1. Mathematics and Statistics

Related courses in mathematics and statistics might cover such topics as:

▶ Probability and statistics

▶ Combinatorial analysis

▶ Abstract algebra

▶ Graph theory

▶ Linear algebra

▶ Numerical analysis

▶ Scientific computation, especially applications of linear algebra and numerical analysis

5.3.3.2. Electrical Engineering

Related courses in electrical engineering might cover such topics as:

▶ Circuit theory and design

▶ Solid state electronics and semiconductor devices

▶ Communications

▶ Control theory

▶ Information theory

5.3.3.3. Physics

Related courses in physics might cover such topics as:

▶ Electricity and magnetism

▶ Solid state physics

▶ Computational physics

5.3.3.4. Psychology

Related courses in psychology might cover such topics as:

▶ Cognitive psychology and information processing

▶ Problem solving

▶ Artificial intelligence

▶ Human factors

▶ Psycholinguistics

▶ Perception

5.3.3.5. Mechanical Engineering

Related courses in mechanical engineering might cover such topics as:

▶ Mechanical linkages, particularly as they relate to robotics

▶ Computer-assisted design and manufacturing

5.3.3.6. Management and Information Science

Related courses and topics in management and information science might cover such topics as:

▶ Operations research, particularly optimization

▶ Economics, especially project scheduling and estimation

▶ Management, especially techniques related to automation and to high-technology development

▶ Role of computers in organizations; how organization structures interact with information flow

5.3.3.7. Public policy

Related courses in public policy might cover such topics as:

▶ Social implications of large-scale computing

▶ Consumer issues in personal computers

▶ Policy issues arising from computing and communications

▶ Computer models for policy analysis

▶ Legal issues such as ownership of software, liability, and security

5.4. Advanced Computer Science

This material is of interest to specialists. Whereas all computer science students would be expected to master much of the material described in previous sections, only students specializing in an area would puruse topics of this section in depth. The depth intended here is at or just below first-year graduate level; as a result this material might form part of a master's degree curriculum. This is not to suggest that we see an undergraduate education as covering the graduate curriculum, but rather that we believe that a senior undergraduate should master that depth in *selected* areas.

The organization given here has been driven by the content of the material; it is not to be construed as a course organization. For example, a course in software engineering might cover much of the material listed under "Systems" and "Process and Design" and also reinforce previous topics in the other areas. Likewise, a course similar to the traditional compiler course might be retained—not to teach compiler building, but to exhibit a medium-sized system with a well-understood structure and to take advantage of the time invested in the example by using it to cover advanced material in data structures, application of formal methods (parsing theory), and interface construction.

Within each of the areas listed below we would expect to find contributions from the traditional areas of theory, software, and hardware. We hope that this organization will avoid inappropriate compartmentalizations. We also hope that it will stimulate thought about the interactions among historically disparate areas and simplify the inclusion of individual topics that haven't grown into course-sized entities.

5.4.1. Control

This area includes scientific and engineering aspects of algorithms, especially as expressed in programs running on computers. Topics such as the function of CPU's, sequentiality and concurrency of processing, use and analysis of algorithms, correctness of algorithms, fault tolerance, probabilistic and heuristic methods are all aspects of control.

Many of these concepts appear repeatedly: for example, the notion of concurrent processing appears in various guises in numerous contexts. These include hardware circuits, interrupts, communication protocols, software synchronization mechanisms such as semaphores and monitors, software process constructs such as coroutines and tasks, database transactions, and operating systems policy for scheduling and allocation.

5.4.2. Data

This area encompasses the manipulation and representation of information, in computation and especially in computer programs. Thus notions of state, physical storage devices, addressing and accessing methods, types, representation, specification, encryption, and "quantity" of information are all included here.

These topics also appear throughout computer science. For example, the notion of naming or addressing appears in hardware addressing (direct, indirect, virtual), memory hierarchies, program variables (scope, extent, binding), operating system storage policies (working sets, overlays, virtual memory management), database models, file directories, and file access methods.

5.4.3. Systems

A system is a regularly interacting or interdependent group of software or hardware modules that forms a unified whole. The study of systems includes the identification, quantification, and management of complexity in systems, the design and construction of large systems, the evaluation of performance, reliability, and security of systems, and how systems are distributed and how communication is performed.

5.4.4. Language

The language area includes the ideas of notation, syntax, semantics and the study of traditional programming languages and their implementation and specification. This area also includes issues of user interfaces, human factors, and technologies such as speech and graphics.

5.4.5. Foundations

The foundations of computer science are concerned with a body of mathematical and theoretical topics, although the importance and applications of these topics are far-reaching in both science and engineering contexts. Sample topics are the study of computability and complexity, logic and semantics, queuing theory, graph theory, and information theory. The study of modelling as a tool for analysis is also included. The ability to formulate and analyze empirical and theoretical models is essential.

5.4.6. Design

This area covers the management of complexity, especially when human behavior or performance is involved. It includes engineering considerations pertinent to development (e.g., readability and maintainability of code) techniques for managing the design and development of large systems (e.g., instrumentation of programs to aid in debugging and performance evaluation) and design criteria for systems (e.g., reliability and human factors). It also addresses the economics of software including creation costs, maintenance costs, and life cycles.

5.4.7. Communications

This area covers topics related to the transmission of information. As computer architectures become more distributed, the transmission of information between them becomes a key feature. Personal and home computers are being used more and more for storing, processing, and sharing information and less for computational purposes. This area includes both the methodologies used to achieve information transmission and the implications of widespread access to information. It also covers methods for preventing such access, i.e., information security.

5.4.8. Applications

These include both applications that depend mainly on ideas from computer science and applications that are important because of their use of computer science material, but that are not computer science in and of themselves. The first category includes applications that are taught to synthesize knowledge from various parts of computer science and present these ideas as parts of a working system. Examples are compilers, operating systems, graphics, and some artificial intelligence programs. The second category includes systems which are rich in their use of computer science techniques. Examples are large financial systems, airline reservation systems, commercial database applications, CAD/CAM systems, remote sensing, and CAI.

6. Program Organization

This chapter presents a set of requirements and a suggested curriculum for a complete undergraduate computer science major. In keeping with our expectations about the responsibilities of future computer scientists, considerable flexibility is provided to allow for professional breadth, and the computer science component places heavy emphasis on fundamental concepts. To this end, a number of electives are specifically constrained to be mathematics courses, a number of electives are specifically constrained to be nontechnical, and a concentration in an area outside of computer science is required. Even if the curriculum is developed as a set of courses without an associated major, this brief discussion of the sort of program that could be based on the curriculum provides a good global perspective.

Section 6.1 tabulates the general requirements for the program. Section 6.2 describes our intentions about the use of electives; it takes the form of advice to advisors. For both philosophical and practical reasons we have allowed considerable flexibility in the choice of electives. We have done this to provide students and their advisors with the opportunity to construct focussed programs tailored to students' interests, not as a sort of permissiveness. Section 6.3 discusses the balance of computer science, technical, and non-technical courses. This balance was established to support the goal of a liberal professional education. To show that the program is actually feasible, Section 6.4 presents a sample four-year program that satisfies both the letter and the spirit of the requirements.

6.1. Requirements

We assume that a normal load is five courses per semester for eight semesters and that college requirements dominate the first year. The distribution of courses in the last three years is roughly 35% to computer science and mathematics, 15% to other technical electives, and 30% to humanities, social sciences, and arts. There is considerable flexibility in the remaining 20%.

We expect that the electives will be used to form focussed, coherent programs; in many cases computer science courses will be coupled to specializations in a non-computer science area. Wise use of electives depends critically on individual advising; electives should be chosen in keeping with an overall plan rather than as isolated decisions each semester. Good use of the electives may be encouraged by publishing examples of approved specializations and providing a review and approval mechanism for individual programs.

A total of 40 courses are required. The distribution is as follows:

Freshman year (controlled by college)		10
Computer Science and Mathematics		10
Specific required courses	4	
Constrained Computer Science (3xx)	2	
Advanced Computer Science (4xx)	2	
Constrained Mathematics courses	2	
Technical courses		5
Nontechnical courses (Humanities, Social Sciences, and Fine Arts)		9
Electives outside the Computer Science Dept		6
Non-CS Concentration		—
[constructed from other electives]		
Total		**40**

The elective structure of this program provides considerable flexibility for adapting the program to individual goals and to joint degrees.

The specific requirements for the program are as follows:

▸ *Freshman Requirements (10 courses):* At most schools, college requirements will dominate the freshman year. This design therefore reserves space for a year's worth of courses required by the college (including both technical and nontechnical courses). Although this delays the student's entry into computer science courses, it preserves flexibility for selection of a major at the end of the freshman year. We expect that for students likely to enter computer science the freshman courses will typically include

PROGRAMMING AND PROBLEM SOLVING [110],
DISCRETE MATHEMATICS [150],
CALCULUS I AND II [MATH 121 AND 122],
PHYSICS I [PHYS 121],
one other course in natural sciences, or engineering
one course in writing
one course in history or social science
two other courses

We believe that the five courses not named should be broadly distributed, so we make no additional constraints.

▸ *Computer Science and Mathematics (10 courses in addition to freshman requirements):* Four specific computer science courses are required in addition to the ones in the freshman core:

FUNDAMENTAL STRUCTURES OF COMPUTER SCIENCE I [211],
FUNDAMENTAL STRUCTURES OF COMPUTER SCIENCE II [212],
REAL AND ABSTRACT MACHINES [240],
ALGORITHMS AND PROGRAMS [330].

Four more courses (with some constraints) must be taken within the computer science department, and two courses (again constrained) must be taken within the mathematics department. These include:

> One 300-level system or software course (from TIME AND RESOURCES [310], PROGRAM ORGANIZATIONS [313], LANGUAGES, INTERFACES, AND THEIR PROCESSORS [320]).

> One 300-level theory or approved mathematics course (from FORMAL LANGUAGES, AUTOMATA, AND COMPLEXITY [350], LOGIC FOR COMPUTER SCIENCE [351], NUMERICAL METHODS [MATH 369].)

> Two 400-level computer science courses.

> Two mathematics courses (from COMBINATORIAL ANALYSIS [MATH 301 / CS 251], OPERATIONS RESEARCH I [MATH 292], LINEAR ALGEBRA [MATH 341], NUMERICAL METHODS [MATH 369], MODERN ALGEBRA [MATH 473], LARGE-SCALE SCIENTIFIC COMPUTING [MATH 712 / CS 453], PROBABILITY AND APPLIED STATISTICS [STAT 211 / CS 250]).

▸ *Technical Courses (5 courses after the freshman year):* These may be selected from courses in science and engineering departments plus selected technical courses in other departments. They may include courses in the Computer Science Department.

▸ *Nontechnical Courses: Humanities, Social Sciences, and Fine Arts (9 courses in addition to freshman requirements):* Some of these courses are presumably constrained by college and university requirements. In addition to those requirements, three courses are constrained as follows:

> POLICY ISSUES IN COMPUTING [EPP 380 / CS 380],

> A writing course in addition to the freshman writing requirement,

> Another course with a substantial writing component.

▸ *Electives (6 courses):* Electives are to be selected to support objectives established jointly by the student and his or her advisor. These six electives must be chosen from outside the Computer Science Department.

▸ *Non-CS Concentration:* A concentration of at least three related nonintroductory courses in an area other than computer science is required. Some possibilities will be recommended; students may propose others for approval. Although the concentration may be in the mathematics department, mathematics courses taken as part of the Computer Science and Mathematics requirement may not be used to satisfy the concentration requirement.

Although most of the discussion here has dealt with bachelor's degrees, the curriculum would also support a master's degree. The 4xx courses provide master's-level depth; we believe that undergraduate students should achieve this depth in one or two areas. A master's program would require more breadth at that level, and it would also require a master's thesis. We have not addressed the question of whether specialized topics such as software engineering are suitable programs for a master's degree; certainly such explicit specialization is more appropriate at the master's level than at the bachelor's level.

6.2. Advice on the Use of Electives

The design of a degree program might take either of two forms. The course sequence and requirements could be so tightly constrained and highly specified that a strong program is guaranteed. The disadvantage of this style is that only the variations anticipated by the designers are likely to be accommodated by the program in any reasonable way. As an alternative, the requirements could be left sufficiently flexible that many different strong programs can be constructed. The weakness of such a flexible approach is that inadequate programs also become easy to construct.

We have decided in favor of flexibility in this design because we feel that the field of computer science is still so fluid that we cannot accurately predict what it will look like in a decade. The price of this decision is that the responsibility of the advisor in helping design the individual course of study is increased. The faculty advisor must spend considerable time with each advisee, understanding his strengths, weaknesses, and interests and providing firm guidance to ensure that each computer science major receives an excellent education. This will only work if the number of students is small in relation to the advising faculty. If individual advisors are responsible for too many students, the flexible alternative may not be feasible. In that case it would be necessary to specify allowable programs more rigidly.

Because of the cross-disciplinary nature of computer science, every computer science major ought to have significant exposure to advanced material in some field other than computer science. For that reason we have introduced the requirement for a non-CS concentration, a sequence of at least three non-introductory courses in any other field. This concentration may be in a technical or non-technical field. We imagine that the main areas that will be selected are electrical engineering, mathematics, and psychology, but we also want to encourage students to consider concentrations in fine arts, humanities, the social sciences, the physical sciences, business, or any other area offered at an advanced level by the university. As a result of our commitment to this breadth, our specification of a computer science major has substantially fewer specific requirements than many other majors at Carnegie-Mellon. However our intention is to provide a more rigorous, not a less rigorous, overall program.

We intend that most students take more mathematics than is required in the proposed program. Combinatorial analysis, linear algebra, operations research, numerical methods, graph theory, probability, and statistics are all extremely valuable in many areas of computer science and are commended to the attention of students and advisors.

The typical undergraduate program, as we envision it, draws approximately two-fifths of its content from computer science and mathematics, one-fifth from other technical areas, and two-fifths from humanities, social sciences, and fine arts. This appears to be considerably broader than many of the existing technical and engineering majors at Carnegie-Mellon; we feel that this is appropriate. We expect the number of introductory courses taken to be fairly small. In particular, we strongly discourage the kind of "breadth" that comes from intellectual dilettantism, particularly when the symptom is a plethora of introductory survey courses.

6.3. Program Flexibility

The goal of this curriculum design is to encourage a liberal program containing a well-balanced mixture of courses: technical and non-technical, computer science and non-computer science. We also believe that a computer science major should have the flexibility to embrace a a variety of programs designed to meet the needs of the individual student. The diagram below presents an abstract view of how the mix of computer, technical, and non-technical courses can be varied within the requirements listed in Section 6.1. The *computer science*, *technical*, and *non-technical* sections of the diagram represent the minimum requirements for each section of the curriculum, and the *non-CS* section can be filled by either technical or non-technical courses.

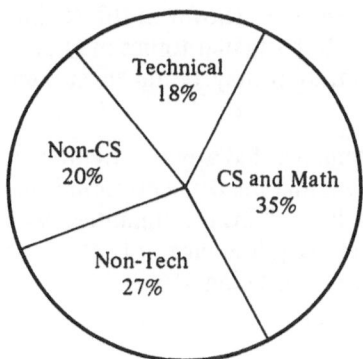

Figure 6-1: Distribution of Requirements in Undergraduate Curriculum

The set of computer science courses can expand to consume the technical electives, but neither the non-technical nor the non-CS courses can be diverted to computer science courses. Thus a valid program must contain between 14 and 21 courses in computer science and mathematics. Similarly, the non-CS requirement can include both technical and non-technical courses, allowing for between 7 and 15 technical, non-CS courses, and between 11 and 19 non-technical courses.

In order to show the limits of the variability in course mixture, the following table shows the course counts for three valid extreme programs: a program containing the maximum number of computer science classes, a program containing a maximum of technically oriented, non-CS courses, and a program containing as few technical courses as possible.

Classification	CS Program	Technical	Non-technical
CS and Math	21	14	14
Technical, non-CS	8	15	7
Non-technical	11	11	19
Totals	40	40	40

The course requirements allow a great deal of flexibility in designing an individual program; at least 45 percent of the total course load (18 out of 40 courses) may be allocated to any one of these three classifications (computer science, technical, and non-technical). Nonetheless, breadth of study is encouraged, since a minimum of 18 percent of the course load (7 out of 40 courses) must be allocated to each classification.

6.4. Sample Program

To show the feasibility of this program, we show a plan for scheduling the program. This plan should be interpreted as one way, but certainly not the only way, to schedule courses into semesters and to satisfy requirements. Naturally, courses may be reordered as long as prerequisite requirements are satisfied. In particular, electives shown in the senior year may be exercised earlier, courses restricted to particular topics may be taken in the senior year, and the non-CS concentration may be taken at some time other than that shown here.

In this sample program, we have recommended a balanced selection of electives. We assume here that the concentration is in engineering or science; it could equally well be formed from humanities, social sciences, or fine arts electives. The actual requirements of the program would permit considerable deviation from this plan.

Freshman		Sophomore		Junior		Senior	
Fall	Spring	Fall	Spring	Fall	Spring	Fall	Spring
CS 110 Program'g & Prob. Solving	CS 150 Discrete Math	CS 211 Fundamental Struc I	CS 212 Fundamental Struc II	CS 330 Algorithms & Programs	CS 3xx Theory or Math	CS 4xx	CS 4xx
Math 121 Calculus I	Math 122 Calculus II	CS 240 Real&Abstr Machines	Math 301 Combinatorial Analysis	CS 3xx System or Software	CS 3xx	Math 3xx	CS 4xx
Phys 121 Physics I	Freshman Science or Engineering	Stat 211 Prob & Statistics	Science or Engineering Elective	◄──── Non CS Concentration in Engineering or Science ────►			Science or Engineering Elective
Freshman Writing	Freshman History or Social Sci	Writing Course	Hum&SocSci or Fine Arts Elective	Another Writing Course	CS/EPP 380 Policy Issues in Computing	Hum&SocSci or Fine Arts Elective	Hum&SocSci or Fine Arts Elective
Freshman Elective (Soc Sci)	Freshman Elective (Humanities)	◄──────── Humanities, Social Sciences, and Fine Arts ────────►					

7. Curriculum '78—Is Computer Science Really that Unmathematical?

Anthony Ralston and Mary Shaw

In 1979, Ralston was investigating curricula for discrete mathematics [95] and Shaw was participating in evaluations of Curriculum '78 and the role of mathematics in undergraduate computer science. They combined their notes to form a criticism of the mathematical content of Curriculum '78 that appeared in Communications of the ACM [94]. Some comments on the paper appeared a few months later [69].

If computer science had not yet developed--significantly—as a science in the ten years between Curriculum '68 [1] and Curriculum '78 [3], then perhaps all those people who wondered if computer science was really a discipline would have been correct. In 1968 computer science was searching for but had not yet found much in the way of the principles and theoretical underpinnings which characterize a (mature) science. Ten years later, there is nothing laughable about calling computer science a science. This decade has seen major advances in the theory of computation and in the utility of theoretical results in practical settings. The rapid growth of the field of computational complexity has greatly increased our ability to analyze algorithms. And perhaps most significantly, we have finally started to make real progress in developing principles and theories for the design and verification of algorithms and programs.

Are these changes evident in Curriculum '78? Sadly, no. That curriculum only lends support to the (incorrect) equation

$$Computer\ Science = Programming$$

that is mistakenly believed by so many outside the discipline. In the "Objectives of the Core Curriculum" [3] only the second objective—"be able to determine whether or not they have written a reasonably efficient and well-organized program"—recognizes that good programming requires more than just mastery of the syntax and semantics of a programming language. And even here the reference to principles and theory is, to be charitable, vague.

The principles and theories of any science give it structure and make it systematic. They should set the shape of the curriculum for that science, for

▸ only in that way can they provide a framework for the mastery of facts, and

▸ only in that way will they become the tools of the practicing scientist.

This is as true for computer science as it is for mathematics, for the physical sciences, and for any engineering curriculum. Inevitably, for any science or any engineering discipline, the fundamental principles and theories can only be understood through the medium of mathematics. In the following sections we focus on the place of mathematics in the computer science curriculum and try to show how badly Curriculum '78 fails in this respect.

But first we note one matter of crucial importance which makes an emphasis on principles and theory even more important in computer science than in other disciplines. Computer science is an evolving field. Specific skills learned today will rapidly become obsolete. The principles that underlie these skills, however, will continue to be relevant. Only by giving the student a firm grounding in these principles can he or she be protected from galloping obsolescence. Even a student who aspires only to be a programmer needs more than just programming skills. He or she needs to understand issues of design, of the capability and potential of software, hardware, and theory, and of algorithms and information organization in general.

	(Curriculum '68)		(Curriculum '78)
M1	Introductory calculus	MA1	Introductory calculus
M2	Mathematical analysis I	MA2	Mathematical analysis I
M2P	Probability	MA2A	Probability
M3	Linear algebra	MA3	Linear algebra
B3	Introduction to discrete structures	MA4	Discrete structures
B4	Numerical calculus		
	plus two of		(Required for some students)
M4	Mathematical analysis II		
M5	Advanced multivariate calculus	MA5	Mathematical analysis II
M6	Algebraic structures	MA6	Probability and statistics
M7	Probability and statistics		

Figure 7-1: Required Mathematics Courses in ACM Curricula

7.1. Curriculum '78 and Mathematics

A comparison between the mathematics content of Curriculum '78 and that of Curriculum '68 is instructive. It reveals that

1. Whereas Curriculum '68 required the student to take eight (8) mathematics courses (see Figure 7-1), Curriculum '78 requires only five (5) mathematics courses.

2. The mathematics courses in Curriculum '68 formed an integral part of its prerequisite structure (see Figure 7-2). Note, in particular, for how many courses the discrete structures course (B3) is a prerequisite. In Curriculum '78, however, there is no mathematics prerequisite for any undergraduate computer science course with the exception of three advanced and clearly quite mathematical courses (only one of which

has a computer science prerequisite). True, Curriculum '78 notes that the "mathematics requirements are integral to a computer science curriculum even though specific courses are not cited as prerequisites for most computer science courses." But this was clearly an afterthought, not present in the preliminary publication [2], and added only in response to criticism of the preliminary version.[2] Moreover, if the mathematics courses are not prerequisite to the computer science courses, the latter cannot teach or use formal techniques that require mathematical literacy.

3. The mathematics emphasized in both curricula is traditional, calculus-based continuous mathematics. In both curricula the only course which is not a common part of the undergraduate mathematics curriculum is a single course in discrete structures.

More generally, the attitudes of Curriculums '68 and '78 toward mathematics are very different. Whereas the authors of C68 aver that "an academic program in computer science must be well based on mathematics since computer science draws so heavily upon mathematical ideas and methods," the authors of C78 say only that "An understanding of and the capability to use a number of mathematical concepts and techniques are vitally important for a computer scientist." The later, too, was an afterthought since the preliminary report stated that "it was recognized in the process of specifying this core material that no mathematical background beyond the ability to perform simple algebraic manipulation is a prerequisite to an understanding of the topics." And note that this "core material" consists of *eight* courses including one on Data Structures and Algorithm Analysis.

One would have to conclude that the authors of Curriculum '78 believe that

1. Mathematics is less important in the computer science undergraduate curriculum today than ten years ago.

2. Basic computer science courses have less need for mathematical prerequisites today than ten years ago.

3. The mathematics that is appropriate for computer science undergraduates has changed not at all in general flavor over the ten-year period between the two curricula.

We think all three of these propositions are wrong, and dangerously so. In the next section we will indicate why and how we would modify Curriculum '78.

---

[2]We think a comparison of the sections devoted to mathematics in the preliminary and final versions of Curriculum '78 clearly imply a "quick fix" which does not address the substantive issues.

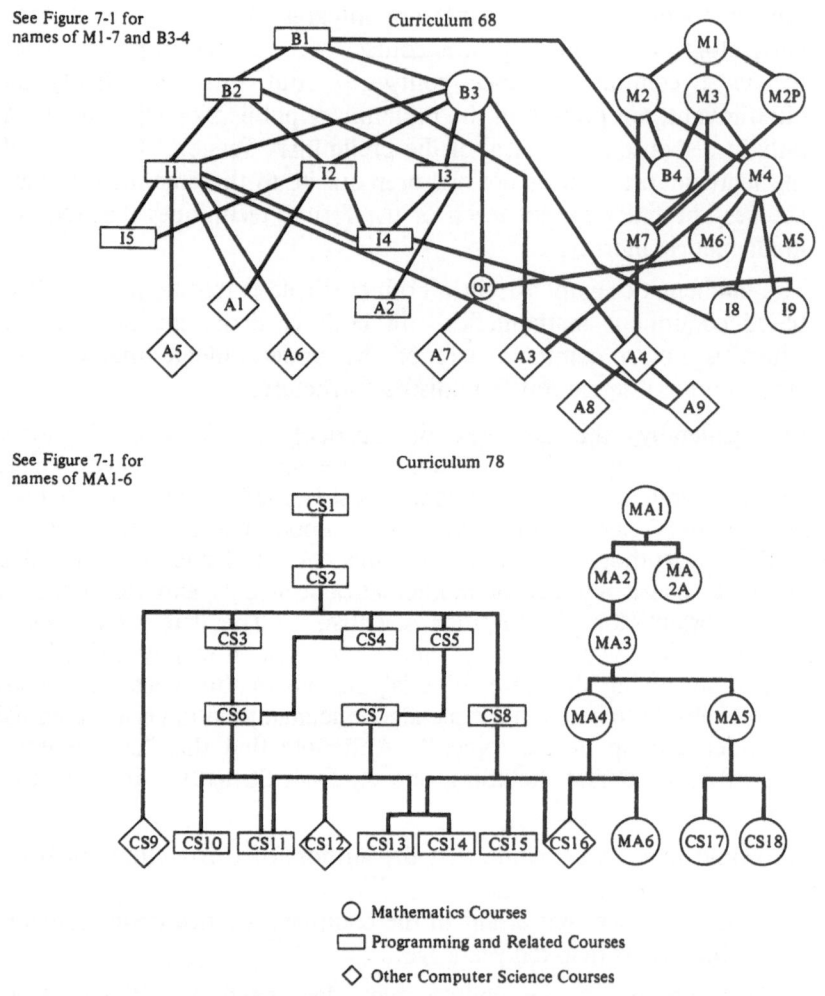

Figure 7-2: Prerequisite Structure for ACM Curricula

7.2. Mathematics for Computer Scientists

A key sentence in C78, also not in the preliminary version, states that "Ideally computer science and mathematics departments should cooperate in developing courses on discrete mathematics which are appropriate to the needs of computer scientists." But, as if to emphasize that this recognition of the importance of discrete mathematics was only an attempt at a quick fix in response to criticism of the preliminary proposal, C78 goes on to say that "Until such time as suitable courses become readily available, it will be necessary to rely on the most commonly offered mathematical courses for the mathematical background needed by computer science majors." And the report goes on to recommend the five courses listed in Table 7-1, four of which are standard undergraduate mathematics courses from a 1965 report of the Committee on the Undergraduate Program in Mathematics (CUPM) [25] and the fifth is "a more advanced course in discrete structures than that given in C68." In other words, instead of going back to the drawing board and doing the mathematics portion of C78 properly, the authors elected to fudge the issue with pretty words and no substance.

For, of course, the quotation in the first sentence of the previous paragraph is correct and should have been the basic philosophy which informed the entire C78 report. In rather more detail this (and our) philosophy is:

1. Mathematical reasoning does play an essential role in all areas of computer science which have developed or are developing from an art to a science. Where such reasoning plays little or no role in an area of computer science, that portion of our discipline is still in its infancy and needs the support of mathematical thinking if it is to mature. Large portions of software design, development, and testing are still in this stage.

2. The student of computer science must be encouraged to use the tools and techniques of mathematics from the beginning of his or her computer science education. This means, for example, that even in the very first course in computer science (e.g., CS1 in C78 where, among other things, the student is to be introduced to "algorithm development") the basic ideas of the performance and correctness of algorithms and their associated mathematics need to be introduced or assumed from a parallel or prerequisite course.[3]

3. The mathematics curriculum for the computer science student must be designed to

   ▶ provide, either in separate courses or within a computer science course, the mathematics prerequisites appropriate to the computer science curriculum. (Obvious, no? But signally missing from C78.)

   ▶ more generally, develop mathematical reasoning ability and mathematical maturity so that students will be able to apply more and more sophisticated mathematics to their computer science courses as they progress through the computer science curriculum.

---

[3]The authors of C78 are, of course, quite correct in not making MA1, Introductory Calculus, a prerequisite for CS1; the problem is that MA1 is the wrong first mathematics course for computer science students.

Some other, more pragmatic, points are worth making before we discuss the mathematics curriculum for a computer science major in more detail:

1. Only the quite basic courses can be required for all students. Depending upon the emphasis and areas of specialization in the last year or two, one set of mathematics courses rather than another may be most appropriate.

2. The needs of the practicing computer professional rather than those of the research computer scientist should be uppermost in consideration of appropriate mathematics for the undergraduate curriculum. To the extent that these needs are different—it is not obvious that they are—the future researcher will have to satisfy his/her needs through undergraduate electives or in graduate school.

3. Although we believe strongly that the values of a liberal education should infuse any undergraduate program, our focus here is on the professional needs of the computer scientist, not on the general education needs. Thus, it may be true that all educated men and women should be familiar with the essence of calculus but it does not *necessarily* follow that computer scientists have a significant professional need to know calculus.

What then is an appropriate sequence of mathematics courses for the computer science major?

1. *Discrete Mathematics.* The overwhelming mathematical needs in the courses which normally comprise the first two years of a computer science major are in areas broadly covered by the rubric discrete mathematics—elementary logic, inductive proof, discrete number systems, basic combinatorics, difference equations, discrete probability, graph theory, some abstract and linear algebra, etc. We believe a two-year sequence can and must be developed (by mathematicians. if possible, but without them, if necessary) for computer science majors. This sequence should be *integrated* with the first two years of the computer science curriculum. Beyond the subject matter itself, we believe that such a sequence would be able to develop mathematical literacy and maturity at least as well as the classical two-year calculus sequence.

2. *Calculus.* A year—but perhaps only a semester—of calculus in the junior year would be appropriate for all or almost all computer science majors. The techniques of calculus have just enough application in standard undergraduate computer science courses to make this desirable. Note also that a year of calculus at the junior level could cover quite a bit more material than a year of freshman calculus.

3. *Statistics.* A basic knowledge of statistics is essential to almost all areas of professional work in computer science. It is not, however, entirely

clear to us whether or not an adequate course in statistics can be taught to computer science students without a calculus prerequisite. If not, then at least a semester of calculus would be mandatory for computer science students.

Much more could be said about possible mathematics courses for computer science students but we shall not do so here. Rather our aim is to urge that the ACM Curriculum Committee on Computer Science go back to the drawing board, make a real study of the mathematics needs of a computer science curriculum, and emerge with recommendations which will have the respect and support of the computer science community.

The mathematics of central importance to computer science has changed drastically in the ten years from C68 to C78. The lack of recognition of this in C78 will undoubtedly lessen the impact of the entire report. Mathematics is at least as important to computer science today as in 1968. But the 1965 recommendations of CUPM are singularly inappropriate to the needs of computer science today.

8. Mathematics Curriculum and the Needs of Computer Science

William L. Scherlis and Mary Shaw

In the summer of 1982, the Sloan Foundation conducted a workshop on the curriculum for the first two years of college mathematics. Scherlis and Shaw were invited to contribute a paper on the relation between computer science and mathematics, especially the support that computer science needs from the mathematics curriculum [101]. The paper is included here to elaborate the nature of our dependence on mathematics.

Although computer science is not a proper part of mathematics, it nonetheless relies heavily on mathematics for its foundations and its methods. Computer science education must depend on the mathematics curriculum for specific ideas and techniques from discrete mathematics, for an understanding of mathematical modes of thought, and for a genuine appreciation for power of abstraction. This paper is a examination of these needs, intended to initiate discussion of the implementation of appropriate mathematics curriculum.

8.1. Some Words about Computer Science

Computer science is concerned with the phenomena surrounding computers and computation; it embraces the study of algorithms, the representation and organization of information, the management of complexity, and the relationship between computers and their users. Computer science is like engineering in that it is largely a problem-solving discipline, concerned with the design and construction of systems. But the computer scientist, like the mathematician, must be able to make deliberate use of the intellectual tools of abstraction and of analysis and synthesis. The relationship between computer science and mathematics is very close and has been discussed at length in the literature. Two very interesting examinations of this relationship are presented by Arden [24] and Knuth [62].

Computer science is a mathematical discipline—so much so that the boundary between computer science and mathematics is often quite hard to pin down. While both disciplines are concerned primarily with abstract structures, computer science is not simply a branch of mathematics. It relies on skills, attitudes, and techniques derived from mathematics, but it is concerned not so much with proofs and the existence of structures as it is with algorithms and the design and organization of structures. In this sense computer science is an engineering discipline. Like engineering, it is pragmatic and empirical and is concerned with the selection, evaluation, and comparison of designs for implementation. But in computer science this study is focused on the behavior of systems such as algorithms, computer organizations, and data representations—that is, on abstract rather than on concrete systems.

This paper addresses the mathematical component of a good undergraduate computer science curriculum. It begins by describing the general nature of the mathematical needs of computer science undergraduates and then discusses some specific mathematical topics that are particularly helpful in computer science education. These mathematical topics include not only traditional mathematical subjects that can be taught in self-contained courses, such as discrete mathematics, but also certain mathematical *modes of thought* that pervade computer science thinking and that cannot be taught easily on their own. In the last sections we consider the impact of these needs on the curriculum.

8.2. Mathematical Aspects of Undergraduate Computer Science

There is a persistent misconception that computer science consists merely of writing computer programs and that, as a result, the education of a computer scientist consists merely of training in skills related to coding and debugging computer programs. On the contrary, the discipline embraces principles and techniques for the design, construction, and analysis of a wide variety of complex systems. Even programming, to be successful, requires the careful application of scientific principles.

Since the principles of computer science are largely mathematical, computer science curricula must necessarily rely on support from mathematics. The traditional mathematics and applied mathematics "service" curricula, steeped as they are in continuous mathematics, do not, however, provide adequate support for computer science. The demands of computer science on mathematics are in many respects quite different from the demands of traditional scientific or engineering disciplines. The most important difference is that, to a much greater extent than in other disciplines, *abstraction* is an essential tool of every computer scientist, not just of the theoretician. The computer scientist is not simply a user of mathematical *results*; he must use his mathematical tools in much the same way as a mathematician does.

A computer science undergraduate curriculum must attempt to develop in the student an appreciation of the power of abstraction and an ability to discover abstractions suitable to new situations. This ability is what mathematicians call *mathematical maturity* (see [108] for further discussion). Mathematical maturity will not be fostered if mathematics is taught to computer science students as a mere skill or as an unpleasant necessity.

Like other scientific and engineering disciplines, computer science must also teach certain specific attitudes, skills, and techniques from mathematics. In computer science, most of these come from *discrete mathematics*—the mathematics dealing primarily with discrete objects. Discrete mathematics as an independent subject is a relatively new arrival, however, and present courses in this area often do not have the cohesion or intrinsic interest of the traditional calculus or algebra sequences. It is interesting, however, that many discrete mathematics courses use the notion of algorithm—a concept from computer science—as their unifying element [95, 107, 114].

8.2.1. Mathematical Modes of Thought Used by Computer Scientists

The most important contribution a mathematics curriculum can make to computer science is the one least likely to be encapsulated as an individual course: a deep appreciation of the modes of thought that characterize mathematics. We distinguish here two elements of mathematical thinking that are also crucial to computer science and speculate on how they might be integrated into a mathematics curriculum. These elements tend not to fall into identifiable courses, but are generally transmitted *culturally*, as part of the process of attaining that elusive quality of mathematical maturity. The two elements are the dual techniques of *abstraction and realization* and of *problem-solving*.

8.2.1.1. Abstraction and Realization

Computer scientists usually deal with situations that are too complicated to understand completely at one time. The chief tool for managing this complexity is *abstraction*—a process of drawing away from detail or selectively ignoring structure. Conversely, complex real systems are built from abstract characterizations by the inverse process of *realization* or *representation*—the selective introduction of underlying structure.

In mathematics, the deliberate use of abstraction is most noticeably manifest in the notion of *mathematical system*. The mathematical systems that are most useful to mathematicians, such as groups, fields, or categories, are those that best focus recurring problems. In computer science this kind of abstraction or encapsulation appears in many forms. Finite-state automata, for example, permit study of control flow in programs without reference to variables or data.

Mathematics can be characterized by its search for gems of abstraction—those abstractions that capture the essential qualities of a phenomenon and ignore the rest. Computer scientists carry on a similar search, but, because the structures they describe usually become manifest as real systems, they are concerned with the *performance* of systems as well as with their functional properties. Consequently, computer scientists find they are often fighting two sides of the same battle: Given a complex problem, they must develop abstractions that provide a way of managing the complexity, allowing for clear and effective reasoning about the problem. But they must also ensure that the representations or realizations that are hidden beneath their abstractions yield implementations with satisfactory performance.

The computer scientist who appreciates the variety of mathematical systems will be better able to evaluate structures and organizations for program and system design. A student who becomes comfortable thinking in terms of systems will be more likely to appreciate the full generality of the program or system structures he creates and less likely to think only in terms of the present specific application.

To strike the best balance between clarity and performance, the computer scientist needs a large and varied arsenal of abstraction and realization techniques. Some of these are rooted in conventional computer science and are therefore most appropriately taught in the context of computer science problems. Others, however, are best transmitted through a comprehensive study of mathematical reasoning.

One of the most powerful tools for abstraction is *language*. For example, programming languages are languages that allow the expression of algorithms without reference to particular realizations of algorithms in computer hardware. These languages also give us a way of describing data by means of its structure, not by its representation as "bits" in a computer memory. Like mathematical languages, computer languages are not designed in a purely *ad hoc* fashion; they are, rather, manifestations of carefully chosen lines of abstraction. If a computer science student is to appreciate the variety and universality of computer languages, he or she must have a mathematician's understanding of the nature and use of language. This includes, for example, understanding the nature of symbols and the essence of deduction—carrying out worldly reasoning by means of symbol manipulation.

This discussion does not, alas, point to courses from "traditional" computer science curricula [3, 54] that will satisfy this need. (Indeed, the standard curriculum designs barely acknowledge the fact that exposure to mathematical reasoning is appropriate for computer science [94, 95].) There are courses in mathematics, however, that can foster the kind of understanding we seek. A good logic course, giving a kind of introspective view of mathematical reasoning, can be of great benefit to the computer scientist. Other mathematics courses, such as the analysis courses that are intended for mathematicians (as opposed to the ones intended for calculus "users"), can be of value simply because of the experience in mathematical definition and reasoning that the students obtain.

8.2.1.2. Problem-solving

Computer science is a problem-solving discipline, concerned with the development of cost-effective solutions (such as programs and machines) to computational problems. Computational problems do not in general have predictable structure and are almost always stated in abstract terms. As a consequence, the construction of programs (or even machine architectures) is analogous to the construction of mathematical proofs. While a proof (or program) has a well-defined structure, the process of obtaining it can be quite undisciplined, involving all sorts of peripheral and heuristic knowledge. Thus, the computer scientist, like the mathematician, must have command of a variety of problem-solving techniques, and must be able to apply them in a creative and yet disciplined fashion.

The designers of many graduate curricula in computer science have acknowledged the importance of abstract problem solving and have incorporated problem-solving workshops based on such texts as [92] into their programs. We suggest that this need should be directly addressed in undergraduate curriculum design [115]. It is very important for students to be aware of the problem-solving process and of the general techniques that they can apply to it. Courses on these topics have been offered in engineering and computer science departments using texts such as [99, 122], but they could be equally appropriate in mathematics departments.

8.2.2. Discrete Mathematics

In addition to the ability to think like a mathematician, a computer scientist requires fluency in some specific areas of mathematics. These are the areas usually (collectively) called discrete mathematics, and they include such topics as elementary set theory and logic, abstract algebra, and combinatorics. Since this material is well-understood, an outline should suffice:

- ▶ *Elementary Set Theory and Logic.* It is important that the treatment of logic go beyond the usual manipulative knowledge of the propositional connectives and quantifiers. Students should have an appreciation of the central issues of mathematical logic and in particular of the role of language in mathematical definition and reasoning. This appreciation can be brought out both in the subject material *per se* and in the way it is presented.

- ▶ *Induction and Recursion.* These are recurring themes in computer science and should be covered in depth; induction underlies nearly all techniques for reasoning about the correctness and performance of programs.

- ▶ *Relations, Graphs, Orderings, and Functions.* This is a part of basic mathematical fluency. Without this knowledge, it is hard to understand even the most basic algorithms.

► *Abstract Algebra.* Algebraic structures recur in computer science, particularly in automata theory, complexity, software specification, and coding theory. A good introduction to algebra will develop in the student an understanding of the notion of mathematical system and will give him experience in using several of the more common ones.

► *Combinatorial Mathematics.* Analysis of algorithms requires a wide variety of mathematical skills; these are drawn mostly from combinatorial mathematics and from probability and statistics.

Although we have not as yet found a completely satisfactory text for discrete mathematics in computer science, the books [72, 107, 114] can serve as a starting point.

8.2.3. Continuous Mathematics

Although our primary emphasis here has been on the role of discrete mathematics in the computer science curriculum, we believe that continuous mathematics is also important to the education of a computer scientist. A mathematician's calculus course can serve as an excellent introduction to mathematical thinking. We will need to consider the question of when calculus should appear in the curriculum. For the purposes of computer science courses, discrete mathematics should appear as early as possible, preferably in the freshman year, but it has also been argued that calculus should precede discrete mathematics in the mathematics curriculum.

8.3. Some Remarks about Computer Science and Mathematics Curricula

As we noted above, the undergraduate computer science curriculum designs currently endorsed by major professional organizations have very weak mathematics requirements [3, 54]. Perhaps this is only a side-effect of the recent rapid growth of undergraduate computer science, but in any case it is widely viewed as a shortcoming. (See [94] and reactions to that article [69].) It is interesting to note that *earlier* computer science curriculum designs [1] contained much stronger mathematical requirements. Comparisons of the early and recent curricula are given in [94, 95].

With respect to the mathematics curriculum, we believe that support for the ideas and topics listed here would not cause major disruption to most mathematics curricula. The most significant change would be the addition of a freshman- or sophomore-level course in discrete mathematics. We believe that this course would be beneficial to students in other departments as well as to computer scientists. (The case for teaching elementary discrete mathematics to all students is presented by Ralston in [95].) Beyond that, most of the material we propose is fairly standard, though perhaps different in emphasis from in the traditional mathematics service courses. We should note here that our list should in no way be construed as complete; we mention topics only to provide an indication of the kind of material that is relevant.

Although much of the material computer scientists need is already provided in standard courses, we believe that both computer science and mathematics curricula would be strengthened by recasting some of those courses a bit. Teachers of mathematics can take advantage of their students' knowledge of computers by showing how classical techniques are realized in computational systems and, where appropriate, by drawing on the rich collection of practical examples supplied by computer science. Linear algebra and numerical analysis courses already do this, teaching computational techniques along with abstract definitions. Discrete mathematics, combinatorics, and graph theory courses also often make extensive use of programming exercises. These programming exercises give students an unusual "hands-on" way of experimenting with abstract structures. Moreover, Lochhead [73] argues that programming *per se* contributes to understanding mathematical ideas.

8.4. Conclusion

Computer science as a discipline has reached the point where there is enough intellectual substance for undergraduate degree programs to be meaningfully offered. Computer science courses are no longer simply programming "service" courses offered for the benefit of computer users; there is truly fundamental conceptual material to be imparted.

A successful undergraduate curriculum, in which basic principles are set forth and elucidated, can only come about after intensive self-examination in the field. Naturally enough, there is a certain lag between the time these principles first emerge and the time they can be effectively integrated into a curriculum, but we feel that there is now a consensus among computer science researchers and practitioners regarding the mathematical content of the field, as sketched in this paper. This consensus, unfortunately, does not extend to the methods for imparting the mathematical material; this remains one of the central challenges of computer science and mathematics curriculum design.

9. Theory and Practice in the Fundamental Computer Science Course

The fundamental computer science course in this curriculum is the two-semester sequence FUNDAMENTAL STRUCTURES OF COMPUTER SCIENCE I AND II [211/212]. Fundamental Structures was originally designed in 1974 and 1975, and the original lecture notes evolved to a textbook based upon the course [127]. In 1978 William A. Wulf, Mary Shaw, Paul N. Hilfinger, and Larry Flon prepared two papers about the course [36, 50]. This chapter incorporates extensive material from these two papers along with new information based on more recent offerings of the course.

Traditionally, the first two programming courses have emphasized basic techniques and skills—the details of a programming language, basic problem solving and program development, "structured programming," the manipulation of simple data structures and files, basic sorting and searching algorithms, etc. They have placed little or no emphasis on such "advanced" or "theoretical" material as rigorous specification and verification, formal language definition, automata, or performance analysis. Their approach, in other words, is similar to that taken by elementary calculus courses, which teach the mechanics of differentiation and integration without bringing in too much theoretical material. The reason for avoiding theory in an elementary calculus course is quite legitimate: for most students, rigorous treatment is not useful enough to justify spending time on it at the expense of manipulative skills.We shall argue here that this reasoning does *not* apply to programming.

If computer programming is to become an "engineering discipline," computer science students must acquire the tools for rigorous analysis and evaluation of programs. An early course in the undergraduate curriculum should introduce the fundamental principles of the discipline, just as freshman calculus teaches the basic analysis skills for most engineering disciplines. The course described in this chapter teaches mathematical principles and practical programming applications in a unified form.

9.1. Introduction

The typical undergraduate computer science program begins with introductory courses in programming, computer organization, and data structures. Subsequent courses in comparative languages, compilers, programming methodology, and systems programming contribute to a student's programming ability. Although students are generally required to learn some theory (e.g., discrete mathematics and automata theory) they rarely appreciate, as undergraduates, the relationships between the theoretical foundations of computer science and the programming process.

Yet the study of the programming process has come to be known as "software engineering." The term "engineering" is not used lightly, but to convey the idea that good software can be constructed only through the application of sound scientific principles that lead to simple, understandable structures, cost effectiveness, and reliability. Since engineering is the application of science, software engineering should be the application of computer science. How, then, can software engineering be properly taught if students do not understand the underlying principles?

FUNDAMENTAL STRUCTURES OF COMPUTER SCIENCE I AND II [211/212], taken by students after they have completed an introductory programming and a discrete mathematics course, is the course in this curriculum that expose undergraduates to theory at the same time as relating that theory to programming. It is a prerequisite for most other computer science courses. It integrally includes not only topics from conventional second and third computer science courses (data structures, "structured programming", programming language details, etc.), but also basic theoretical material. These topics include automata and formal languages , formal specification of algorithms and data types, complexity analysis, program and data abstraction techniques, and program verification. Naturally, we introduce these topics at an elementary level. Nonetheless, they form the central organizing core of the course. In a sense, this course is as much about reading programs as it is about writing them. The course has been offered in various forms for ten years, and our experience shows that most students *can* handle the more advanced material.

Some important benefits have resulted. First, students become familiar with important mathematical tools, including logic and sets, induction and recursion, and the concepts of formal proof and mathematical model. Although the familiarity is one of manipulative ability rather than deep theoretical understanding, it is nonetheless quite valuable as a foundation.

Second, this course teaches important prerequisite material for more advanced courses. For example, a course on compilers needs the concepts of grammar and finite state automaton, rather than a deep theoretical understanding of them. Since the concepts of state and state transition are important to other aspects of programming, we now introduce them much earlier. The instructor of a compiler course may find a brief review in order, but the emphasis can be placed on lexical analysis and parsing, not on automata themselves.

Third, because practical and theoretical topics are presented together, it is easier to show how the same ideas reappear in different forms in different areas of computer science.

Overall, our principle motivation is the conviction that programming should be an engineering discipline, and that engineering disciplines must be grounded in *science*. Further, to be effectively taught, this science must be introduced as early as possible.   In contrast to the measure-theoretic underpinnings of the calculus, the theory we introduce is both comprehensible and immediately instructive to working programmers.   In addition, the topics we cover are fundamental to later courses.   By introducing the topics early in the curriculum, we provide a common vocabulary for these later courses, eliminate redundant treatment of topics, and give students greater exposure to the material and a better chance to absorb it.

Finally, the existence of abstract, theoretical ideas in FUNDAMENTAL STRUCTURES OF COMPUTER SCIENCE I AND II [211/212] will help to locate students who are unlikely to master the curriculum early in their education—while they still have time to pursue other more appropriate fields.   This screening function occurs other areas (e.g., chemistry, physics) and is unpleasant but necessary.

9.2. Course Overview

Unquestionably, FUNDAMENTAL STRUCTURES OF COMPUTER SCIENCE I AND II [211/212] is a course intended to teach students to program well. Although it contains much theory, the theory is never isolated from programming examples.   The course is organized around the broad concepts of *control*, *data*, and the *interaction of control with data*.   Each concept is treated from several different viewpoints.   These are, sequentially,

1. theory

2. programming language issues

3. representation

4. reasoning.

Although later sections of this paper illustrate this treatment of the concepts, we should emphasize points 3 and 4: representation and reasoning.   These are key programming issues that are often overlooked.

Theory is related to practice in the course by introducing *abstract* ideas that are *represented* by (less abstract) *structures*.   Thus, data is discussed first in terms of data types, values, and the relations between inputs and outputs of functions.   Particular data structures are then presented as examples, and implementations are treated as concrete representations of the abstract definitions.   Thus the presentation of stacks first explains the concept and the operations (e.g., push, pop), then discusses the choice of a linked list or an array as the representation.   Similarly, control structures are first discussed in terms of their abstract behavior, but then brought down to machine-level representations (e.g., tests, transfers, and related addressing).   As a result, students should acquire the ability to use the structures present in any particular language, without losing sight of the abstract model (the "structured program") they should strive for.

Having knowledge of the representations available to him (for both control and data), a programmer needs the tools that will help to choose the best one. We refer to this as *reasoning about programs*. Reasoning takes (at least) two forms—reasoning about *performance*, and reasoning about *correctness*. A representation (i.e., a program segment or data structure) must be *validated* and *analyzed for efficiency*. Thus faced with two seemingly reasonable (performance-wise) choices, a programmer should opt for the one that is more obviously correct. Faced with two different yet correct algorithms, he should be able to recognize the more efficient one. To do this, he must have some knowledge of the meaning of correctness and an understanding of both basic complexity ideas and time-space tradeoffs.

Finally, the scientific ideas that have been presented and illustrated with small examples are brought together in the solution of larger problems. These extended examples, which may be thought of as engineering studies, are detailed developments that produce working programs. Most are short (about 5 pages) but a few become multi-week projects in which students write longer (about 10 to 30 pages) programs that require the integration of a few separate ideas. Students are sometimes asked to use, evaluate, and modify the resulting programs to come to grips with nontrivial implications of the theory.

The material presented in the course comes from a wide range of topics, but it can be incorporated into three categories: fundamental structures of control, fundamental structures of data, and interaction of data and control.

These headings illustrate our view that data/control duality issues should be the basis for both programming language design and program development. For each of the three major parts above, we discuss (as previously mentioned) mathematical models, programming language representations of the models, underlying representations of language constructs, and reasoning about both correctness and performance. In the next section of this paper we outline the major sub-topics.

The course assumes a prior introduction to programming in a language like Pascal, and some background in discrete mathematics (set theory, logic, boolean algebra, functions, relations, mathematical induction). Nonetheless, it has been necessary to teach some programming language features (e.g., use of pointers) and to review some particular topics in discrete mathematics.

9.3. Major topics in the Fundamental Structures Course

In the following sections, we discuss the particular topics we have covered, giving our reasons for including each. We are not attempting to outline the entire course here, and the reader should refer to the course outline in sections 11.2.1 and 11.2.2 for a more comprehensive description of the topics.

9.3.1. Models of Computation: Automata

FUNDAMENTAL STRUCTURES OF COMPUTER SCIENCE I AND II [211/212] introduces abstract models of computation and several of the standard models: the finite-state machine, the push-down automaton, and the Turing machine. The discussion provides a framework in which to discuss models in general and their use in understanding abstract properties of programs. For example, we discuss the relative power of programming constructs, and show how one can perform such comparisons having suppressed unessential details. Finite-state machines also provide a setting in which we can introduce nondeterministic computation early and gently.

In practical programming terms, the finite-state machine is the skeletal prototype of the table-driven computation. In some instances, FUNDAMENTAL STRUCTURES OF COMPUTER SCIENCE I [211] course, has taken students through the construction of a table-driven lexical analyzer. Traditionally, lexical analysis is the subject of a compiler course, but an applications programmer who wishes to write sophisticated input routines may well find the technique useful.

Knowledge of automata is of obvious use in later courses on compilers and in understanding sequential logic design. In particular, we find it convenient for students to have seen the concept of the *state of a computation* and of state transition before going on to a compiler course.

9.3.2. Formal Languages

At an elementary level, the study of formal languages provides two descriptive notations: regular expressions and BNF. Not only are these useful in defining the syntax of programming languages (and hence, in reading programming language definitions), but they are convenient and succinct notations for describing many other notations: program input formats, for example.

As specification tools, both BNF and regular expressions have the advantage that there are well-established techniques for obtaining implementations (parsers) from the specifications. Even without delving into the theory of parsing, FUNDAMENTAL STRUCTURES OF COMPUTER SCIENCE I AND II [211/212] course still lays much of the groundwork for these constructions by surveying the correspondences between automata and grammars. When the lexical analyzer example mentioned in the previous section is used, it is specified using regular expressions. This specification guides the construction of the tables.

BNF provides many examples of recursive definition. Thus, it serves as one introduction to the topic of recursion (and certainly a more motivated introduction than the recursive factorial function). The structure of a simple recursive descent parser follows naturally from recursive definition to recursive implementation.

9.3.3. Formal Specification and Verification

One of the most important lessons to be learned in any introductory programming sequence is the distinction between specification and implementation—between what is to be done and how it is to be accomplished. Our own experience as programmers indicates just how important this distinction is; we cannot *conceive* of large programs until we rise above the details of their construction. At the same time, our teaching experiences also show that the idea of rigorously specifying a program apart from its implementation and the concomitant practice of using the specification of a routine rather than its code to understand its effect, are among the most difficult things to teach undergraduates. Hence, we consider it vital to stress rigorous specification and the distinction between specification and implementation as early and as often as possible.

Therefore, FUNDAMENTAL STRUCTURES OF COMPUTER SCIENCE I AND II [211/212] introduces the use of mathematical entry and exit assertions for program and procedures. Besides their utility as a specification device, these have the pedagogical advantage that the student is forced to abstract and to write a general statement of the effects of his program, since it is extremely awkward to encode the workings of a program in its entry and exit assertions. As the course now stands, most of the practice that students get in using formal specification comes in the units on data types.

We cannot expect students to become proficient in the art of program specification as a result of this course alone. It is a difficult art, requiring experience and, ideally, a certain mathematical tastefulness for its successful practice. This is true even when the specification language is precise English (as it often must be) rather than mathematical notation; the difficulties of producing good documentation are well known. Nonetheless, we have observed in later courses that our students have started thinking in terms of the abstract effects of their programs.

Having introduced program specification, we next consider verifying the correctness of an implementation with respect to a specification. Again, it would be impossible to expect the students to be really proficient at programming verification. However, by showing that it is *possible* to argue rigorously and systematically about various properties of a program, we hope the students will be more inclined towards rigor in the programming process. Whether or not one believes that detailed formal program verification is feasible in practice, it is still valuable to acquire the habit of verifying programs *informally* and of constructing them to make that task easier. We can show, for example, that not only does the proper modularization of a program into routines make them more readable, but it also simplifies formal and informal reasoning—verification conditions become smaller.

Standard treatments of verification tend to stress mechanical manipulation—the generation of verification conditions. It is true, furthermore, that such concrete skills are easier to teach (if harder to motivate) than general methodological principles. Still, teaching the general principles, such as "rigorous program construction," is really our global aim. The purpose of introducing program verification at all is simply that a program is generally cleaner, simpler, and more likely to be correct if it is well thought out and carefully constructed. Even if a student never again formally verifies a program, simply understanding that it *can* be done can change the ways he thinks about programs and programming.

9.3.4. Algorithmic Analysis

Cost analysis is a critical activity in any engineering discipline. Programming is no exception. From personal experience, we know that careful *quantitative* analysis of program cost is all too rare. Many programmers "optimize" programs only at the "put as much as possible into registers" level, rather than at the algorithm level, and have no good idea of where their programs can actually benefit from optimization.

Therefore, FUNDAMENTAL STRUCTURES OF COMPUTER SCIENCE I AND II [211/212] introduces some simple cost analysis techniques. It discusses the notion of the *order of complexity* of a computation, and the distinction between the shape of a cost curve and its actual values. All of this material is rather obvious, of course, but until it is pointed out that cost analysis might be interesting, programmers tend not to do it. By introducing students to the subject formally, we get them in the habit of making implementation decisions on the basis of expected costs, and to develop in them an ability to do informal performance estimates. We need hardly mention that these techniques and attitudes are useful in any later course on the analysis of algorithms.

9.3.5. Data Types

As we mentioned above, FUNDAMENTAL STRUCTURES OF COMPUTER SCIENCE I AND II [211/212] subsumes the usual data structures course. However, its treatment of data structures differs from what we observe to be the conventional treatment. Traditionally, individual data structures are introduced in close association with their standard representations. In keeping with current methodology, as well as our policy of *separating* specification from implementation, this course first introduces the general concept of a *data type*. That is, we define a data type in terms of the legal operations and the essential observable behavior of those operations. We go on to show how to specify this observable behavior rigorously, and to use the data types thus described, without mentioning how the operations are implemented.

Having developed the tools needed to describe data types, we introduce many standard data types in terms of their abstract properties. Later, and separately, we discuss standard implementation techniques. Our separation of the specification of an abstract type from the concrete implementation allows us to explain several alternatives and discuss their relative merits. Depending upon the particular time the course has been taught, the section on implementation techniques has varied in comprehensiveness; recently, it has included list, tree, and graph representations, and reasonably complex algorithms for their manipulation. Incidentally, the algorithms involved in manipulating these representations provide good opportunities for illustrating the formal methods of the previous sections.

The *separation of concerns* behind this approach has proved valuable in developing large software. As was the case with the specification of procedures, however, novice programmers initially have difficulty understanding that a data type has an abstract behavior distinct from its implementation. This only suggests to us that they should start getting used to the idea early in their programming education.

We have found a fairly simple exercise that illustrates the distinction between specification and implementation. We first asked the students to provide the implementation of a simple data type (e.g. *stack*) using a particular representation (e.g. the standard vector representation). Next, we asked them to write a main routine implementing a simple algorithm that uses data of this type (e.g. an iterative routine to convert Polish notation to infix form). They were to code this algorithm using only the abstract specification of the data type (e.g., using a linked list representation) without modifying a single character of the main routine.

This exercise, simple as it seems (and *stack* is the archetypal "toy" data type), proved quite useful in illustrating the point of data type abstraction. It is particularly convenient if the course uses a language like PASCAL or Modula II, but it is possible in other languages.

To illustrate further the separation of specification and implementation, the syllabus for FUNDAMENTAL STRUCTURES OF COMPUTER SCIENCE II [212] includes a short section on Lisp. In it, students re-implement certain data standard data types in a rather different language. We should be able to evaluate the value of this action following the next version of the course.

9.3.6. Recursion

At least one paper [76] argues that recursion is not simply an esoteric device, but a programming tool that can facilitate algorithm development. Instances crop up quite naturally, such as recursive descent parsing from a BNF definition, which we mentioned earlier. One important class of instances is the set of divide-and-conquer algorithms, whose natural descriptions are recursive. Several sorting algorithms, for example, have a high-level divide-and-conquer description. Finally, of course, recursively defined data structures (such as trees) are most naturally manipulated recursively.

In FUNDAMENTAL STRUCTURES OF COMPUTER SCIENCE I AND II [211/212], we try to present what might be called "recursive thinking"—the art of seeing a problem in terms of smaller instances of itself. It is its own formal verification method. One simply assumes (inductively) that all recursive calls behave according to specification and shows that the arguments of recursively nested calls get progressively "smaller." This kind of reasoning occurs throughout a course on algorithm design or compiler design. Its early presentation therefore serves as important preparation for this and other more advanced courses.

Recursion is another place where the specification and implementation of a program may differ. We may specify a program recursively, but implement it as an iterative program (perhaps with a stack). For example, merge sorting has a very simple recursive definition, although its usual implementations are iterative and interleave the recursive calls. This brings up the whole subject of program development by successive transformation. The similarity between simple push-down automata and simple recursive programs, in particular the fact that one may use either to recognize context-free languages, provides one starting point for such a discussion. This topic is one that we will cover in a future version of this course.

9.3.7. Programming Exercises

As mentioned, many programming exercises are assigned throughout the course. These complement the lecture material and provide an opportunity for the students to apply the material presented in lecture. As the course progresses, the programming assignments become somewhat longer and more involved.

Near the end of the course, we have recently assigned a rather large (4 week) programming project. It has typically been a small relational database system in which students must support both hashed and tree storage structures. To emphasize the distinction between specification and implementation, the database is introduced to students as a complex abstract type, which must be implemented with different representations to facilitate different types of queries. The assignment also exercises students' understanding of binary tree and hashing algorithms. The amount of code required and the difficulty the students have in managing the project (even with the help of the course staff) provides good motivation for study in the more advanced software engineering classes.

9.4. Experiences

Over the last ten years, the bulk of the material above has appeared, with varying relative weights on the topics, as part of FUNDAMENTAL STRUCTURES OF COMPUTER SCIENCE I AND II [211/212]. (Again, we call the reader's attention to the course outline in sections 11.2.1 and 11.2.2.) The course also involves a considerable amount of classical data structures material and requires a considerable amount of student programming. Close to a thousand students have taken the course under many different instructors, usually during the sophomore year.

Perhaps the natural reaction, or at least the one we hear from some colleagues, is that the course is too rigorous, too "formal", and too voluminous for its sophomore audience. Students, however, are generally favorable. Of course, some students do not master all of the material; but they benefit from an introduction early in their education. Perhaps the sheer volume of material most complicates the teaching of the course. Even in two semesters, there is a lot to cover.

9.5. Conclusions

Recent advances in the field of programming languages and methodology have made it clear that a student who intends to be a computer scientist or software engineer needs training in the fundamental ideas of theoretical computer science as well as a solid background in the design, construction and analysis of programs and data structures. FUNDAMENTAL STRUCTURES OF COMPUTER SCIENCE I AND II [211/212] is designed to present the concepts in such a way that theoretical and practical ideas complement each other.

The topics we discuss in the course contain nothing that we don't use ourselves as programmers. The course also provides a common basis for later courses, which in itself is useful. Nonetheless, we do not view the course as a particularly radical departure from the *subject matter* of other curriculum proposals. We do think it is an important re-ordering of the material. It is an attempt to present basic principles together in one course and to teach these principles *before* their use in more advanced courses. Thus, just as an introductory engineering course teaches mechanical before structural design, we have put the science and mathematics of programming *before* most of the actual coding.

We have tried to present a set of theoretical topics which we believe to be valuable in the practice of software engineering. We have tried to argue that students should learn these topics as early as possible. In short, we want to promote the notion of programming as an engineering discipline employing scientific and mathematical methods.

10. Remarks on the Design

The curriculum presented here departs from traditional curricula in a number of ways. Further, some of our objectives do not appear explicitly in the design. This chapter presents remarks about the curriculum that may help the reader to interpret and evaluate it.

10.1. General Philosophy

We believe that previous computer science curricula have been too compartmentalized. They contain many courses focused on specific areas, but offer little or no overview of the material. We attempt to organize courses by coherence of the content, not necessarily following traditional boundaries. We also attempt to blend theory and practice in virtually all courses. We believe that a strong emphasis on recurring themes (e.g. abstraction and reliability) will help to bridge the gaps between topics that, on the surface, may seem unrelated.

Though we stress foundations and unifying concepts, we also intend to teach students to appreciate and produce specific solutions to specific problems. We realize that in many respects this is best achieved by exposing students to a wealth of examples of good engineering solutions and by providing large amounts of supervised hands on experience of the sort that lectures and examinations simply can not provide.

We also feel that the goal of liberal professional education is best served by breadth. An undergraduate who overspecializes can graduate unable to learn on his own, and unable to communicate his knowledge to laymen. We believe that specialization can and should happen after graduation, whether the student enters the work force or graduate school. Our goal is to produce an individual with a broad base on which to build additional knowledge, not a worker with skills that may be obsolete shortly after graduation.

Certain themes run throughout the curriculum and are discussed in Chapter 5. Although these topics are not mentioned explicitly in most courses, all carry the responsibility to convey those ideas through their tone and examples.

We strongly feel that a curriculum for computer science must have support from current technology. Software support for undergraduate courses is essential. Section 3.2 discusses this in more detail. Students must have convenient and substantial access to computer resources. This access is vital. Computer technology can also be applied in more enterprising applications than those common today. In addition to routine applications, computers can be used in creative settings; examples include teaching via intelligent, advice-giving programs, and other kinds of computer-aided instruction. Extensive experience with current technology at this early stage will prepare the student for the real programming world.

10.2. Relation to Traditional Courses

Many of the concepts of computer science appear in nontraditional contexts in this curriculum. This is often because older courses were organized around artifacts such as computers or software systems, whereas our design tends to be organized around ideas.

As a particular instance, there are no courses specifically about operating systems or compilers. Both of these traditional courses take as an integrating theme a complex system such as a compiler or operating system from which most of the main ideas are naturally motivated. This curriculum, however, organizes these topics by grouping similar abstract ideas. As a result, the major concepts from an operating systems course appear in TIME AND RESOURCES [310], COMPUTER ARCHITECTURE [440], and BIG DATA [410]. The topics from traditional compiler and comparative languages courses are distributed through LANGUAGES, INTERFACES, AND THEIR PROCESSORS [320], TRANSDUCERS OF PROGRAMS [420], and ADVANCED PROGRAMMING LANGUAGES AND COMPILERS [421].

FUNDAMENTAL STRUCTURES OF COMPUTER SCIENCE I AND II [211/212] is the introductory sequence for computer science students. It replaces what is usually a second programming course with one that introduces many important concepts (abstraction, representation, correctness, performance analysis) as early as possible. It also has a significant programming component. This sequence has been taught at Carnegie-Mellon for several years, and we are very satisfied with it as an introduction to computer science and a foundation for further study.

Early courses usually deal with building programs from individual statements, while a software engineering course (e.g. SOFTWARE ENGINEERING [413]) deals with the interaction of whole modules in a complete system. A new course, PROGRAM ORGANIZATIONS [313], is intended to cover the intermediate stage. Its emphasis is on the common frameworks for building modules from code fragments.

Two courses in this curriculum are descendants of traditional courses, but with a significant shift in emphasis. REAL AND ABSTRACT MACHINES [240] is an introduction to hardware that includes relevant material from programming systems and automata theory with the explicit intention to bridge the normal distances between those areas. ALGORITHMS AND PROGRAMS [330] is an algorithms course with a highly pragmatic bent—blending the more usual Abstract Algorithms and Advanced Programming courses.

Several of the intermediate courses are derived from traditional courses with modest changes in emphasis. These include FORMAL LANGUAGES, AUTOMATA, AND COMPLEXITY [350] and INTRODUCTION TO ARTIFICIAL INTELLIGENCE [360].

10.3. Course Organization and Style

By longstanding tradition a *course* is a series of lessons long enough to fill a semester and containing a reasonable amount of intellectual content. The honor accorded by tradition should not be permitted to mask inadequacies of the course format; nor should skepticism be permitted to destroy the well-reasoned product of our predecessors. This curriculum focuses on the course as the atomic unit of instruction, not because of a blind devotion to tradition, but because we found no compelling alternative. Our commitment is to excellence in instruction of the next generation of computer scientists, not to the provision of particular courses or degrees.

We are not certain that every aspect of computer science education is best served by the traditional course structure. Alternatives to the traditional emphasis on the course include the Oxford/Cambridge tutorial model, various work/study programs, and the competency examination model. The conventional course orientation of the curriculum should be seen as an interim solution, realizing that some concepts may be best taught via organizations not yet imagined.

Computer science courses often resemble physics laboratory courses in their need for direct observation and manipulation of the phenomena of computer science. Consequently, computer science courses depend on laboratory facilities and staff to create and operate those facilities; including machines, working space, and programmers. They also require numerous development tools, libraries of examples, and instructional software.

Parallels can also be drawn to literary criticism courses, where students learn to write by reading the writing of others. This example supports the belief that people can best learn to program by reading programs. Thus courses involving reading good example programs might be very productive.

More difficult is the challenge of teaching those lessons that by their very nature span more than the semester duration of a traditional course. The true value of good programming practice and detailed documentation are learned only when a programmer has to modify a program months or years after he has written it, a situation that most students never face. It may be possible to design a sequence of courses requiring the student to examine or use his previous programs to motivate the need for these habits.

Two brief notes on mechanics: Firstly, our prerequisite structure is intended to be strictly observed. We recommend that a letter grade of "C" or better be required to satisfy a prerequisite. Secondly, we feel classes should be restricted to a manageable size. The report of the 1980 CMU Computer Science Undergraduate Program Committee [118] recommended the following limits on the size of course sections: 50-60 students in second year courses (2xx) and 20-30 students in upper division courses (3xx and 4xx). These limits were independent of issues related to degrees. We strongly endorse these limits.

10.4. Course Numbering Scheme

A rational system of course numbers provides a quick hint about the level and content of each course. Our scheme is derived from the Carnegie-Mellon system, and is similar to those in use at many universities. The level of a course is the year of the average student taking the course (1xx for freshman courses, 2xx for sophmores, and so on), except that 4xx courses are for suitable for both seniors and graduate students.

A three-digit course number *JKL* is interpreted as follows:

► The first digit *J* indicates the level of the course:

1xx	Basic, introductory, or general literacy
2xx	Elementary computer science
3xx	Intermediate topics focussing on individual ideas
4xx	Advanced or specialized topics integrating individual ideas

► The second digit *K* indicates the general subject matter of the course:

x0x	General
x1x	Systems
x2x	Programming Languages
x3x	Algorithms and Analysis
x4x	Computer Systems; Hardware
x5x	Theory and Mathematics
x6x	Artificial Intelligence and Psychology
x7x	Design, Graphics, and Computer-Aided Activities
x8x	Management, Economics, Policy
x9x	Applications

► The third digit is assigned arbitrarily to distinguish different courses within a category.

In the rest of this document we will often refer to courses offered other than computer science. In some cases, the courses could equally well be offered in either computer science or the other department, and only for historical reasons are they not computer science courses at Carnegie-Mellon. In other cases, the courses are most appropriately offered in the other department. For all of these courses, we will generally use the Carnegie-Mellon course numbers, which do not necessarily adhere to the convention described above. In particular, engineering courses often use an initial digit of 1 for *sophomore* courses and 2 for *junior* courses. Such course numbers are prefixed with a department name (e.g. Math 301). The Carnegie-Mellon courses are unlikely to correspond to course numbers at other schools; they are used here merely to provide unique identification.

11. Course Descriptions

This chapter presents descriptions of the courses we propose to be the major components of an undergraduate computer science curriculum. We have tried to write descriptions that will indicate clearly the scope and emphasis we have in mind. However, a complete course design is a major undertaking, so most of these descriptions should be viewed as design sketches, not full designs. An overview of the course structure, including course names and prerequisites[4], is given in Figure 11-1.

Some courses that are shown may well be offered by departments other than computer science. In some instances (as in COMBINATORIAL ANALYSIS [MATH 301 / CS 251]), these courses have computer science course numbers. Given more time and broader expertise, the Curriculum Design Project would have made detailed sketches on such courses; instead, information about similar courses currently offered at Carnegie-Mellon University has been provided, but only for purposes of exposition and completeness. We are neither endorsing nor criticizing the current curricula of these courses.

---

[4]The prerequisite structure is complete only for computer science courses.

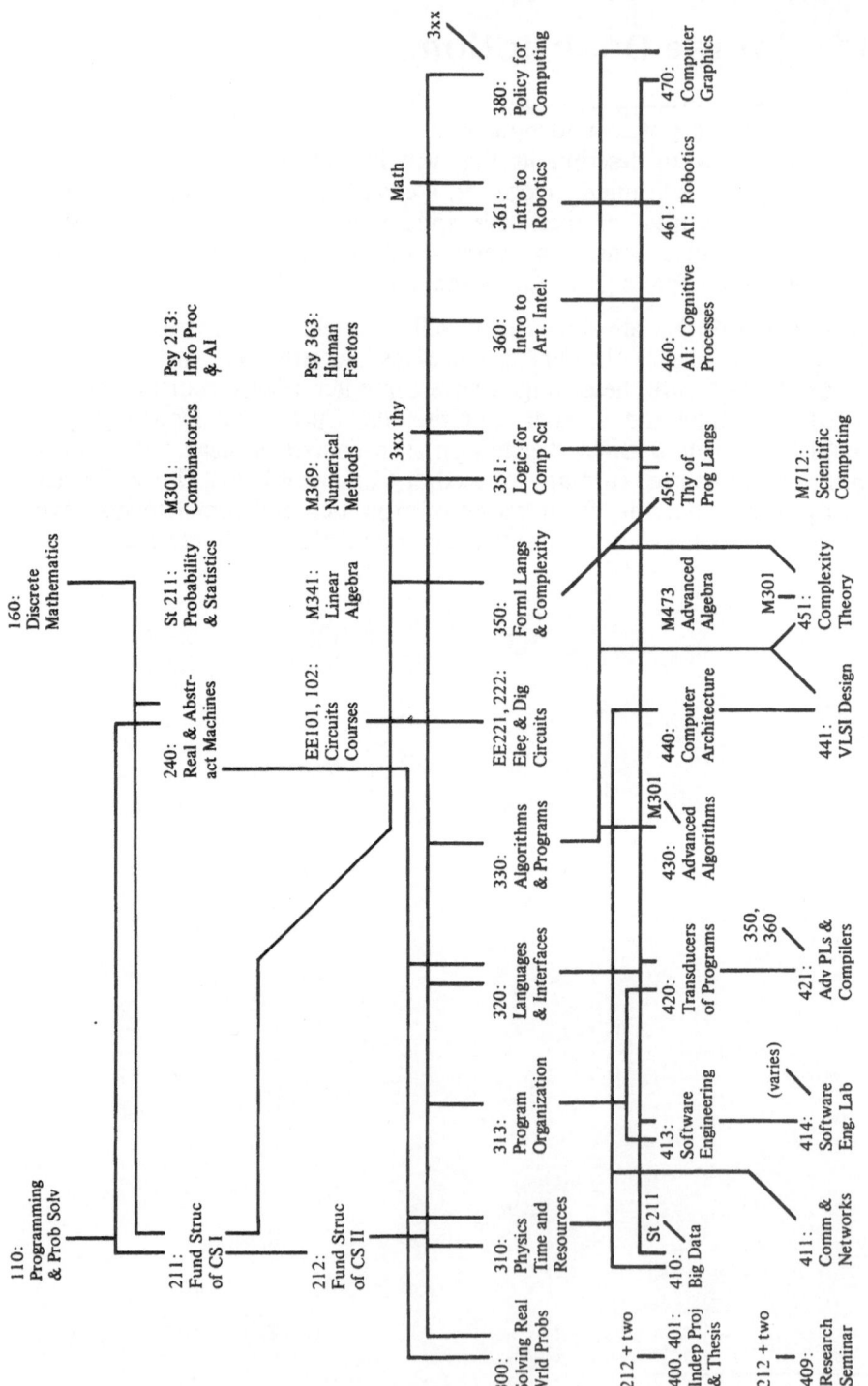

Figure 11-1: Course and Prerequisite Structure

11.1. Basic and Introductory Courses

Introductory computing courses serve all the communities described in Section 3.1. They exist to provide general computer literacy to the campus at large, to provide the background for students who must use computers in other disciplines, and to provide sufficient background for the basic computer science courses.

In order to establish the basis of our computer science curriculum, we give a brief description of two kinds of introductory course. The first of these is directed at the need for general literacy about computing. The second is directed at the need for the specific skills required for good programming, including problem-solving skills. The two courses are independent; we conceive of the former as a universal requirement.

11.1.1. Computers in Modern Society [100]

This course presents algorithmic thinking and the role of computing and technology in contemporary society. It covers

- ► Use of computing facilities, including important classes of programs such as text formatters, electronic message systems, interactive computation and planning systems, and public information utilities.

- ► Survey of classes of computers and applications, with emphasis on the diversity of the applications and the common elements of the successful ones.

- ► The style of precise, deductive reasoning and problem solving that characterizes science and engineering. One of the carriers of this idea will be an introduction to elementary computer programming.

- ► Ethical and social implications of widespread computing power.

There is an opportunity for this to become a course that teaches all students, particularly nontechnical students, about the nature of scientific reasoning. Such a course would include elements of formal logic, history and philosophy of science, and Western civilization. Hands-on experience with computers could provide the direct experience and tangible feedback that is often difficult to provide. The course would help balance the conventional view of liberal education that calls for scientists to take substantive courses in the humanities but not for humanists to take substantive courses in the sciences.

11.1.2. Programming and Problem Solving [110]

Techniques for solving problems with computers, including problem-solving and programming skills. This is the course for students who will take more advanced computer science courses. This course could use an introductory programming text and books such as the following:

- R.G. Dromey, *How to Solve It by Computer* [33].
- J.R. Hayes, *The Complete Problem Solver* [48].
- G. Polya, *How to Solve It* [92].
- M. Rubinstein, *Patterns of Problem Solving* [99].
- W.A. Wickelgren, *How to Solve Problems* [122].

11.1.3. Discrete Mathematics [150]

Prerequisites: NONE

Description: This course introduces and relates a variety of discrete mathematical themes and subjects. This course is intended to serve prospective computer science and mathematics majors, among others.

Objectives: At the end of this course, a student will have a command of the basic ideas and techniques from discrete mathematics and will be able to apply them to problems outside mathematics, such as problems in computer science. Besides these skills, students will have begun to develop an appreciation of the nature and use of abstraction, an understanding of the roles of language and logic in mathematics, an understanding of the notion of mathematical structure, and an understanding of the nature of mathematical proof.

Ideas: This course will be the primary carrier of the following:

- Problem diagnosis
- Abstraction: how to go from particular to abstract
- Representation: making abstract structure concrete
- Mathematical reasoning and the notion of proof
- Operational reasoning and the notion of algorithm
- Recursion and induction; operational vs. relational reasoning
- Modelling
- Synthesis: building mathematical structures

It will reinforce or share responsibility for:

- A precise understanding of the notion of algorithm and an appreciation of the role of algorithms in mathematics.

Topic Outline:

1. **Graphs**
   - Fundamental ideas
   - Directed acyclic graphs and trees
   - Simple algorithms on graphs

2. **Sets**
   - Sets, set membership, and set equality
   - Defining sets: extension and abstraction, paradoxes
   - Relations between sets, operations on sets
   - Infinite sets
   - Relations, mappings, and functions

3. **Logic skills**
   - Propositions and truth functions

- ▶ Individuals, predicates, and quantification
- ▶ The language of propositional and predicate logic
- ▶ Expressing statements in the language of logic
- ▶ Informal deduction in predicate logic

4. Induction

- ▶ Elementary stepwise induction and complete induction
- ▶ Induction over general structure and inductive definitions of sets
- ▶ Recursive definitions (e.g., of sequences and functions)

5. A brief introduction to logic and mathematical reasoning

- ▶ Syntax: formal languages and inductive definitions
- ▶ Deduction: axioms, rules of inference, and proofs
- ▶ Informal and formal proofs
- ▶ A glimpse at semantics: interpretations and soundness

6. Counting

- ▶ Combinations, permutations
- ▶ Binomial and multinomial theorem
- ▶ Inclusion/exclusion

7. Relations, equivalence relations, and order

- ▶ Properties of relations, closures
- ▶ Equivalence relations, partitions, equivalence classes
- ▶ Examples of equivalence relations: divisibility of integers, modular arithmetic
- ▶ Partial and linear ordering
- ▶ Well-founded ordering

8. Retrospective

- ▶ Several lectures drawing on previous work to reinforce the themes of abstraction, proof, algorithm, etc. More than one unit of this type may be needed.

9. Matrices

- ▶ Matrix algebra
- ▶ Linear systems, Gaussian elimination
- ▶ Applications: incidence matrices, transitive closure, Markov chains

10. Algebraic structures

- ▶ Binary operations (associativity, commutativity, transitivity, idempotence, etc.)
- ▶ Semigroups (strings, composition of functions, matrices, etc.)
- ▶ Algebras and structures
- ▶ Monoids, groups, rings, and fields
- ▶ Boolean algebra, propositions, and sets
- ▶ Isomorphism and homomorphism

11. Recurrence relations

- ▸ Recursive definition of sequences
- ▸ Differencing and summation
- ▸ Solution of linear recurrence relations
- ▸ Applications to algorithm analysis (e.g., Fibonacci, binary search)

References:

- ▸ G. Birkhoff and T.C. Bartee, *Modern Applied Algebra* [12].
- ▸ J.L. Gersting, *Mathematical Structures for Computer Science* [40].
- ▸ R. Johnsonbaugh, *Discrete Mathematics* [57].
- ▸ I. Lakatos, *Proofs and Refutations: The Logic of Mathematical Discovery* [65].
- ▸ C.L. Liu, *Introduction to Combinatorial Mathematics* [71].
- ▸ C.L. Liu, *Elements of Discrete Mathematics* [72].
- ▸ D.F. Stanat and D.F. McAlister, *Discrete Mathematics in Computer Science* [107].
- ▸ H.S. Stone, *Discrete Mathematical Structures and their Applications* [109].
- ▸ J.P. Tremblay and R.P. Manohar, *Discrete Mathematical Structures with Applications to Computer Science* [114].

Implementation Considerations and Concerns:

- ▸ Although this is a mathematics course, it should be taught with close attention to the concepts of computer science.
- ▸ This course should provide sufficient maturity for the student to continue with more advanced mathematics courses. If this one term course proves insufficient, it may need to be split into a two term sequence. In that event, course COMBINATORIAL ANALYSIS [MATH 301 / CS 251] would be involved in the redesign.
- ▸ The themes listed as major ideas for the course provide the fabric that holds the course together. Although they are not mentioned explicitly in the subject listing, it is important that they be approached frequently in textbooks and in lectures.
- ▸ We have, as yet, found no textbook that covers all these topics adequately, even for a one-semester freshman-level introduction. The chief problem is inadequate treatment of logic. In the near term, the best way to deal with this problem may be to require two standard textbooks or to supplement a standard textbook with copies of course notes from the instructor.

11.2. Elementary and Intermediate Computer Science Courses

These courses form a core that is germane to nonterminal, terminal, and joint-interest students. We believe that all those students need a foundation based on a balance between theory and practice Divergence, if any, can come in the advanced courses.

In addition to the courses we define here, some of the content of computer science as described in Chapter 5 may be taught in departments other than computer science. These departments include mathematics, electrical engineering, psychology, and others. We have generally avoided designing courses that cover material taught at Carnegie-Mellon in these other departments.

To show more complete coverage of computer science, however, we list here the titles of courses that should be jointly listed by computer science and another department. Catalog descriptions for these courses appear in Chapter 12.

► COMBINATORIAL ANALYSIS [MATH 301 / CS 251]

► NUMERICAL METHODS [MATH 369 / CS 352]

► PROBABILITY AND APPLIED STATISTICS [STAT 211 / CS 250]

► LINEAR CIRCUITS [EE 101 / CS 241]

► ELECTRONIC CIRCUITS [EE 102 / CS 242]

► ELECTRONIC CIRCUITS II [EE 221 / CS 340]

► ANALYSIS AND DESIGN OF DIGITAL CIRCUITS [EE 222 / CS 341]

Some of the courses outlined in this section may also be jointly listed. In particular, DISCRETE MATHEMATICS [150] can be listed in the Mathematics Department and REAL AND ABSTRACT MACHINES [240] is very similar to INTRODUCTION TO DIGITAL SYSTEMS [EE 133].

11.2.1. Fundamental Structures of Computer Science I [211]

Prerequisites: PROGRAMMING AND PROBLEM SOLVING [110]
           DISCRETE MATHEMATICS [150]

Description: This course introduces students to the fundamental scientific concepts that underlie computer science and computer programming. Software concepts such as abstraction, representation, correctness, and performance analysis are developed and are related to underlying mathematical concepts. Students are asked to apply these concepts to programming problems throughout the course.

Rationale: The ideas of abstraction and analysis are fundamental in computer science and should be introduced as early as possible in the curriculum—as soon as students are familiar with the activity of programming. The specific ideas and techniques introduced in this course serve as the basis for detailed development in later computer science courses.

Objectives: At the end of this course, a student will:

- ▶ Appreciate the central role of abstraction in computer science and programming.
- ▶ Be able to realize abstract specifications in concrete programs.
- ▶ Be able to reason precisely about the correctness and performance of simple programs.
- ▶ Understand how a knowledge of analytical techniques can aid informal programming activity.
- ▶ Have improved programming skills through practice and analysis of existing code.
- ▶ Be aware of some of the basic program structures and programming techniques.

Ideas: This course will be the primary carrier of the following:

- ▶ The nature and use of abstraction in computer science.
- ▶ Basic techniques for reasoning about program correctness and analyzing program performance.
- ▶ Fundamental algorithms for searching and sorting in arrays.

Topic Outline:

1. **Introduction: understanding programs**
   - ▶ Abstraction
   - ▶ Specification and implementation
   - ▶ Analysis: correctness and performance
   - ▶ Search in an unordered array
   - ▶ Search in an ordered array: Binary search

2. **Brief review of discrete mathematics for computer science** (review of DISCRETE MATHEMATICS [150])

   ► Logic skills
   ► Sets, relations, functions, graphs
   ► Induction and recursive definition
   ► Abstraction, language, and logic

3. **Finite-state automata**

   ► Alphabets and languages
   ► Describing languages: recognition and generation
   ► The notion of state; abstract automata
   ► Nondeterminism
   ► Regular expressions
   ► Equivalence of models

4. **Programming languages: abstractions and pragmatics**

   ► Syntax: programming languages as formal languages
   ► Flowchart programs and control structures
   ► Basic control structure abstractions: sequencing, conditionals, and iteration
   ► Procedures and function subprograms
   ► Identifiers, variables, binding, and assignment
   ► Parameter binding
   ► Scope, extent, and free-variable binding
   ► Recursion

5. **Programming languages: semantics and representation**

   ► Specifying the meanings of programs
   ► Machine-level languages
   ► Representation of high-level constructs
   ► Translation and interpretation

6. **Correctness of programs**

   ► Program specification and programming language semantics
   ► Test vs. proof
   ► Assertions about programs
   ► Hoare assertions and weakest preconditions
   ► Loops and invariants
   ► Specification, abstraction, and modularity

7. **Performance of programs**

   ► Introduction to concrete complexity
   ► Introduction to instrumentation of software
   ► Resource utilization
   ► Measuring input size, expressing cost

- ▶ Experimental methods for cost estimation
- ▶ Analytic methods
- ▶ When and how to improve performance

8. **Major examples**

- ▶ Abstraction and analysis revisited
- ▶ Sorting
- ▶ Lexical Analysis

References:

- ▶ A.V. Aho, J.D. Hopcroft, and J.E. Ullman, *Data Structures and Algorithms* [6].
- ▶ O.J. Dahl, E.W. Dijkstra, and C.A.R. Hoare, *Structured Programming* [27].
- ▶ W.A. Wulf, M. Shaw, P.N. Hilfinger, and L. Flon, *Fundamental Structures of Computer Science* [127].

Resource Requirements:

- ▶ Compiler and adequate machine access for running programs (e.g. in Pascal)
- ▶ Example programs
- ▶ Interpreters for micro-languages
- ▶ Simulators for finite-state automata
- ▶ Possibly program timing support—routines and test-bed
- ▶ Data sets for sorting and searching—tuned to best, worst cases for various algorithms

Implementation Considerations and Concerns:

- ▶ Students should read programs as well as write them. The instructor should provide a wealth of well-written examples for students to read and modify.
- ▶ See Chapter 9 and papers by the authors of the *Fundamental Structures* text [36, 50] for discussions of the course design.
- ▶ Because of the inexperience of the students and the large class sizes, this course is particularly sensitive to the problem of concentrating on the examples at the expense of the major underlying themes and principles.
- ▶ So as to provide an appropriate bridge from the programming done in PROGRAMMING AND PROBLEM SOLVING [110] to the more theoretical matters that are the topic of this course, it is important to blend in a sufficient number of programming examples.

11.2.2. Fundamental Structures of Computer Science II [212]

Prerequisites: FUNDAMENTAL STRUCTURES OF COMPUTER SCIENCE I [211]

Description: The course is a continuation of FUNDAMENTAL STRUCTURES
OF COMPUTER SCIENCE I [211]. It comprises five major parts: data
abstraction, implementation of data types and corresponding algorithms,
models of computation, topics in computer implementations, and a brief
introduction to LISP. In addition to lectures on these areas, students are
asked to complete a number of programming assignments.

The programming assignments are an integral part of the course. They
are often the first programs that are large enough to force the student to
deal with abstraction (by necessity), and they give the student an
opportunity to apply algorithms and abstraction techniques that are
presented in class. Students are asked to program and think about
programming during the entire course. It is this emphasis that ties the
course together.

Rationale: This course presents a breadth first cut across many topics in
computer science. Taken as a last course in computer science, this course
and FUNDAMENTAL STRUCTURES OF COMPUTER SCIENCE I [211] provide
an introduction to the central topics in the field. Taken as an introduction
to the more advanced courses, this course provides students with material
that is either prerequisite or introductory.

Objectives: At the end of this course, a student will have

- ► Enough programming skill to handle larger programming
  assignments and experience in both Pascal and, to a lesser extent,
  LISP
- ► A basic knowledge of data abstraction and specification techniques,
  and the ability to implement a data structure to support a given
  specification
- ► Some background in computability theory
- ► Some background in the implementation of programming
  languages
- ► Some background in the design and analysis of algorithms.

Ideas: This course will be the primary carrier of the following:

- ► Data type specification and abstraction techniques
- ► Data structure design and analysis, including time-space tradeoffs
- ► The organization of systems via the use of layered abstractions
- ► LISP programming

It will reinforce or share responsibility for:

- ► Data representations and related algorithms

▶ Topics in the implementation of programming languages

▶ Computability theory

▶ Verification techniques

Topic Outline:

1. **Data abstraction.** An example is presented almost immediately, so students can begin to program an abstract data type on their own.

    ▶ Course introduction, abstract data types

    ▶ Abstraction, an example of directories as abstract data type implemented via hashing with linear probing

    ▶ Introduction to formal specification

    ▶ Algebraic specifications, sequences, positive integers as examples

    ▶ Abstract models (strings, queues, sets), verification considerations

2. **Abstract data types, their implementation, and corresponding algorithms.** In general, abstract data types are semi-formally introduced before algorithms and representations are discussed. This material is presented in Pascal. It is specifically not intended that the introduction to LISP be merged with the introduction to data types.

    ▶ Basic programming abstractions

    > Variant records, and Pascal modules (independent compilation)

    > Pointers/references introduced

    > Representation techniques (e.g., packing, encoding)

    ▶ Queues and stacks

    > Stacks, nested abstractions

    > FIFO queues

    > Static implementations; e.g. via arrays

    > Implementations involving single linking, double linking, circular structures

    > Modelling, discrete event simulations

    > Bucket hashing

    > Other uses of queues and stacks

    ▶ Types often implemented with trees

    > Abstractions of sets, directories, symbol tables, priority queues, etc.

    > Introduction to trees and definitions: trees as an abstract type

    > Tree walks, uses of trees, specification of trees, binary tree

    > Inductive proofs of trees, representation of trees

    > Binary search trees, recursive and iterative processing

    > Deletion in binary search trees

    > Balancing trees

> Multi-way trees, 2-3 trees, heaps

> Copying structures with pointers/recursion

> Multi-key retrieval, database queries

> Interval retrieval, iterators

▶ Graph-like types

> Graphs introduced, defined, and exemplified

> Graph traversal, connectedness algorithms

> Graph representations and transitive closure algorithms

> Transitive closure algorithms refined, shortest path algorithms

> Overview of traveling salesman and spanning tree algorithms

3. Models of computation: an introduction.

▶ Turing machines

▶ Other models

▶ Church's thesis and computability

▶ The halting problem and undecidability

▶ Context-free languages and the Chomsky hierarchy

4. Topics in computer implementations.

▶ Introduction to storage allocation

▶ Stack-based storage allocation, static and dynamic scoping

▶ Non-stack-based allocation, freelists, explicit merging of objects

▶ Buddy system allocation, marking in-use objects and garbage collection

5. LISP

▶ Notion of applicative language

▶ Programming environments and interpreters

▶ Use of simple, yet powerful, primitives

▶ The power of recursion

▶ Different implementations of abstractions already seen

References:

▶ A.V. Aho, J.D. Hopcroft, J.E. Ullman, *Data Structures and Algorithms* [6]. Chapters/Sections 1, 2.1-2.4, 3.1-3.2, 5.1-5.2, much of 6 and 7.

▶ O.J. Dahl, E.W. Dijkstra, and C.A.R. Hoare, *Structured Programming* [27].

▶ P.H. Winston and B.K.P. Horn, *LISP* [123].

▶ W.A. Wulf, M. Shaw, P.N. Hilfinger, and L. Flon, *Fundamental Structures of Computer Science* [127]. Chapters 7, 8, 9, 10.1-10.5, 11.1-11.2, 13, 14, 15, 16, 19.

Resource Requirements:

- ► Compiler and adequate machine access for running programs (e.g. in Pascal)
- ► LISP interpreter and adequate machine access for running LISP programs
- ► Library of data types to support many of the assignments
- ► Simulator for Turing Machines
- ► Some assignments can involve students with larger programs by giving them running versions of exemplar programs (whose design was presented in class) and asking for modifications.
- ► Note that FUNDAMENTAL STRUCTURES OF COMPUTER SCIENCE II [212] requires much greater computing resources than FUNDAMENTAL STRUCTURES OF COMPUTER SCIENCE I [211].

Implementation Considerations and Concerns:

- ► See 9 and papers by the authors of the *Fundamental Structures* text [36, 50] for discussions of the course design.
- ► Students should read programs as well as write them. The instructor should provide a wealth of well-written examples for students to read and modify.
- ► It is specifically intended that LISP be taught for approximately the last 20 to 25% of the course and that the data structure material be taught initially in Pascal. There are two reasons: First, one new thing is enough to learn at a time. Second, the students should see the data structures material from two points of view (that is, Pascal and then LISP), and the advantages and disadvantages of both should be made clear.
- ► Feedback to students is important. An extensive grading staff is required to provide substantive feedback to students on their programs with respect to algorithms, abstraction techniques, and general programming style. This is especially true when students are supposed to be learning design techniques that require extensive individual feedback and for which answer sheets do not give enough guidance. This is such a course, and it must be adequately staffed.

11.2.3. Real and Abstract Machines [240]

Prerequisites: PROGRAMMING AND PROBLEM SOLVING [110]
              DISCRETE MATHEMATICS [150]

Description: In this course the student is introduced simultaneously to the theoretical models and the hardware instances of machines that compute. The notions of layers of virtual machines is explored and their realization in various combinations of hardware and software are major themes. Beginning with primitive computations, the mathematical concept of function is used to capture the capabilities of combinatorial digital logic circuits. From that base, finite automata are introduced as tools for understanding, analyzing, and designing finite state machines. After that, Turing Machines and, more appropriately, register machines are introduced and related to the architectures of real computers. Finally, microcode, machine/assembly language, and general-purpose programming languages are positioned in this hierarchy.

The laboratory component of this course will require about three hours of lab work per week and will expose the student to simple instances of some of the machine types covered in the lectures, both through construction and through simulation. Students will simulate instances of several classes of machine and will design and construct simple combinatorial circuits and a simple finite state machine.

Rationale: Conventional teaching of computer architecture doesn't convey the sense that constructable systems can be described and reasoned about formally. While the strict identity between formal models and actual machines ends at the finite automata, there is nonetheless a great deal to be learned from exposure to both the formal models of more powerful machines and to the architectural ideas embodied in real machines. The purpose of this course is to expose students to the design and construction of various kinds of computing devices and to establish that there are formal techniques for reasoning about the mathematical properties of computing machines.

Objectives: At the end of this course, a student will be able to:

- ▶ Understand and describe the relationships between some formal models of machines and corresponding real machines
- ▶ Understand the notion of an interpreter of an instruction set and the layers of abstract machines that are present in all real systems
- ▶ Understand the use of a clock to impose the discrete time abstraction on the continuous time functions of real circuits
- ▶ Understand the circuit family abstraction that permits Boolean algebra to describe the behavior of real electronic devices
- ▶ Design and implement simple finite state machines

Ideas: This course will be the primary carrier of the following:

- ▶ Concept of machine as executor or interpreter of an instruction stream
- ▶ Elementary computer architecture
- ▶ Abstract machines, corresponding languages, and corresponding real machines; notion that there are different kinds of machines with different power and various realizations
- ▶ Virtual machines
- ▶ Discrete time, ordering of events
- ▶ Circuit family abstraction

It will reinforce or share responsibility for:

- ▶ Abstraction and representation
- ▶ Finite-state automata, Pushdown automata, Turing machines
- ▶ Basic design levels of hardware (shared with COMPUTER ARCHITECTURE [440])
- ▶ Notion of algorithm
- ▶ Notion of state
- ▶ Boolean algebra

Topic Outline:

1. Function

- ▶ Theory:
  - > Concept of function
  - > Number systems: representation and arithmetic
  - > Boolean algebra (review of DISCRETE MATHEMATICS [150])

- ▶ Techniques:
  - > Combinatorial circuit design (with hardware lab)
  - > Simulation
  - > Analysis, including simplification
  - > Comparison between discrete logic and VLSI techniques

- ▶ Technology
  - > Logic families (with hardware lab)
    - ≫ Survey of available technologies: power, speed, density
    - ≫ Comparisons, tradeoffs, and applications
  - > Logical building blocks, including PLAs, PALs, ROMs, ALUs
  - > Introduction to physical considerations mixed logic, propagation, fan-in, fan-out, rise time, etc)

2. Finite automata

▶ Theory:

> Regular languages, regular expressions

> Finite-state machines (with hardware lab)

> Combinatorial logic with feedback

> Register transfer level description

> Mealy machines and Moore machines

> Asynchronous sequential circuits

▶ Techniques:

> Sequential circuit design
  ≫ Simulation
  ≫ One-hot versus encoded implementations (with hardware lab)

> Registers and latches (with hardware lab)

> Clocks and discrete time (with hardware lab)

▶ Technology:

> Binary memory elements

> Larger building blocks (counters, shift registers, etc)

> Physical considerations (timing, triggering, race conditions, etc)

3. Pushdown automata

▶ Context-free grammars (with software lab)

▶ Context-free languages

▶ BNF

▶ Related real machines—B5000, HP3000, HP calculators (with software lab)

4. Turing machines

▶ Theory:

> Turing machines (major treatment of Turing machines in FUNDAMENTAL STRUCTURES OF COMPUTER SCIENCE II [212])

> Register machines (with software lab)

> Instruction set processor model

> Von Neumann architecture and the Universal Turing machine

▶ Techniques:

> Data path design and control section design

> Assembly languages and machine code

▶ Technology:

> Memory devices:(RAM, Disk, Tape, etc)

> Memory hierarchies

> Examples of microprocessors and microprocessor interfaces

5. Architecture

- ► The emphasis here is on the layers of virtual machines that appear in a computer design. Students should understand how each layer can be implemented in terms of a lower layer and, in turn, masks details of that layer.
- ► ISP and Executor/interpreter model (with software lab)
- ► Microcode
- ► Machine language (with software lab)
- ► Assembly language
- ► Intermediate language (e.g. Pcode)
- ► Higher level languages and their virtual machines

References:

- ► C.G. Bell, J.C. Mudge, and J.E. McNamara, *Computer Engineering* [8].
- ► M. Minsky, *Computation: Finite and Infinite Machines* [79].
- ► D.P. Siewiorek, C.G. Bell, and A. Newell, *Computer Structures: Principles and Examples* [106].

Resource Requirements:

- ► Finite state machine simulator
- ► Regular expression to FSM converter
- ► PDA simulator
- ► CFG to PDA converter
- ► Turing machine simulator
- ► ISP simulator
- ► Digital electronics lab suitable for building simple digital circuits up to FSMs: TTL parts, breadboards, power supplies, signal generators, switches and displays, oscilloscopes, logic analyzer, etc.

Implementation Considerations and Concerns:

- ► It may be tricky to find faculty with the right mix of interests to teach this course with good balance between hardware, software, and theory.
- ► This course is very similar to INTRODUCTION TO DIGITAL SYSTEMS [EE 133], offered in the Electrical Engineering Department. The content is similar enough that the lab facilities might easily be set up in common and shared.

11.2.4. Solving Real Problems [300]

Prerequisites: FUNDAMENTAL STRUCTURES OF COMPUTER SCIENCE II [212]
                 REAL AND ABSTRACT MACHINES [240]

Description: This problem-oriented course provides students with an opportunity to solve practical problems under the guidance of an instructor. Skills from a variety of areas both within and outside of computer science will need to be brought to bear on class examples and assignments posed as problems by the instructor. The emphasis is on the techniques used in obtaining the solution, rather than the solution *per se.* While proper software engineering techniques will, of course, be expected for all solutions involving software, it should be noted that the emphasis in the course is problem solving, *not* software engineering.

Rationale: Traditional courses provide particular knowledge and skills, but usually the problems posed in such courses focus narrowly on the topic of the course. Rarely does a student encounter a problem with the real-world characteristic of requiring a non-trivial combination of acquired skills. In addition, academic assignments often make broad assumptions that make the task much cleaner than actual problems tend to be. This course should help prepare students for the realistic, thorny sorts of problems that they will have to encounter after graduation.

Objectives: At the end of this course, a student will be able to:

- ▸ Critically examine a task and define the real issues in solving a problem. That is, take an engineering approach to a practical problem.
- ▸ Form a well-organized attack on a problem.
- ▸ Implement a solution, cognizant of possible error or oversight.
- ▸ Evaluate a completed solution, and learn and generalize from it.

Ideas: This course will be the primary carrier of the following:

- ▸ Problem analysis, definition, and decomposition.
- ▸ Coping with external constraints not necessarily inherent in the problem.
- ▸ Application of knowledge and technique in novel ways.
- ▸ Critical evaluation of a finished solution.

Topic Outline:

1. **Basic stages of problem solving**
   - ▸ Problem definition
   - ▸ Plan of attack
   - ▸ Execution of a plan
   - ▸ Check for correctness of solution

    ▸ Evaluation of a finished solution

2. Path to a solution as the desired results

    ▸ Working backwards from a final goal

    ▸ Establishment of stable substructures

3. Reductionism vs. holism

4. Knowledge vs. skill

5. Epistemology

6. Models and modelling

7. Analogies and metaphors

8. Expressing a problem or solution

9. Well-structured vs. ill-structured problems

10. Overcoming conceptual blocks

11. Defining and narrowing a problem domain

12. Reduction to a known problem

13. Partial solutions

    ▸ Giving up on hard cases

    ▸ Approximate results; coping

References:

    ▸ J.R. Hayes, *The Complete Problem Solver* [48].

    ▸ I. Lakatos, *Proofs and Refutations* [65].

    ▸ G. Polya, *Mathematical Discovery* [91]

    ▸ G. Polya, *How to Solve It* [92].

    ▸ M. Rubinstein, *Patterns of Problem Solving* [99].

    ▸ W.A. Wickelgren, *How to Solve Problems* [122].

Resource Requirements:

    ▸ A healthy number of class examples of real problems of an inter-disciplinary flavor.

Implementation Considerations and Concerns:

    ▸ This course is modelled after existing "Analysis, Synthesis, and Evaluation" courses taught in engineering curricula, particularly the course described in [88]. Stanford's graduate computer science course 204 was also studied [20, 119, 63].

11.2.5. Time and Resources [310]

Prerequisites: FUNDAMENTAL STRUCTURES OF COMPUTER SCIENCE II [212]
REAL AND ABSTRACT MACHINES [240]
PHYSICS I (MECHANICS) [PHYS 121]

Description: This course conveys the notion that a computer system is the manager of a variety of resources. The primary issues are resource classes, properties and management policies. One resource, time, is particularly important and the course concentrates on control of temporal behavior in computer systems, both at the hardware and the software level. The f.ndamental issues of synchronization, deadlock, contention, metastable states in otherwise multistable devices, and related problems are described. Hardware and software solutions to time control problems are studied and the similarities between the solutions are exposed. The vehicle for the synthesis achieved in this course is the exploration of at least one instance of a real operating system. This course has a substantial laboratory component.

Rationale: Many systems, such as operating systems, file systems, and database systems, are resource management systems. Every system that involves the control of any finite resource presents the designer with resource management problems and every computer scientist will be faced with such systems many times in his career. Operating systems are particularly rich examples of resource management systems and this course uses operating systems as examples for this reason.

Computer systems, both hardware and software, depend heavily upon synchronization and concurrency control because they deal with implementations in which there is real parallelism. This course makes precise many of the terms (e.g., simultaneous, parallel) that we use to talk about time. We make many implicit assumptions about the temporal behavior of computer systems when thinking about hardware and software. Some of these assumptions are correct, while others are convenient simplifications designed to make intractable problems manageable. There are essential difficulties with our concepts of how systems behave in time, some of which are due to mismatches between our intuitions about time and the reality as modelled by physicists.

Objectives: At the end of this course, a student will be able to:

- ► Understand resources and their classifications.
- ► Understand and apply techniques for using, allocating, scheduling, and naming resources.
- ► Design, implement, and reason about software with synchronization
- ► Design, implement, and reason about hardware synchronization circuits

Ideas: This course will be the primary carrier of the following:

- ▸ Resource classification
- ▸ Resource allocation
- ▸ Naming
- ▸ Concepts of concurrency
- ▸ Concepts of nondeterminism
- ▸ Cooperating processes
- ▸ Synchronization (handshaking, semaphores, monitors, etc)

It will reinforce or share responsibility for:

- ▸ Abstract machine models
- ▸ Combinatorial circuits with feedback, memory circuits
- ▸ Addressing, data representation, and storage

Topic Outline:

In addition to the formal content, this course is intended to teach students how to evaluate systems and ideas.

1. **Resources**
   - ▸ Real time
   - ▸ CPU time
   - ▸ Memory hierarchies
   - ▸ Disk
   - ▸ Logical
   - ▸ Real (e.g., printers)
   - ▸ Pre-emptible
   - ▸ Non-pre-emptible
2. **Resource related activities**
   - ▸ Allocation
     - > Paging
     - > Secondary storage
   - ▸ Synchronization
   - ▸ Scheduling and concurrency
     - > CPU
     - > Paging
   - ▸ **Resource managers**
     - > Spooling
     - > Servers for networks
3. **Prototype resources**

- ▶ Hardware resource—multi-access bus (Unibus)
- ▶ Software resource—buffer readers/writers

4. Time

- ▶ Continuous time, Physics
    - \> D.C. circuits
    - \> Propagation delay
    - \> Transmission lines

- ▶ Discrete time
    - \> Clocks
    - \> Events and orderings on events

- ▶ Simultaneity
- ▶ Concurrency
- ▶ Formal models
    - \> Nondeterministic automata
    - \> Temporal logic
    - \> Linear time
    - \> Branching time

5. Hardware and time

- ▶ Handshaking, synchronization
- ▶ Synchronous, asynchronous, self-timed circuits
- ▶ Indivisible operations (test and set, compare and swap, etc.)
- ▶ Metastable states and deadlock
- ▶ Clock generation and distribution
- ▶ Multiprocessor organization
- ▶ Interrupts
- ▶ Interfacing and data communication protocols

6. Software and time

- ▶ Transactions and atomicity
- ▶ Deadlock, livelock—dining philosophers
- ▶ Time clocks
- ▶ Cooperating processes
- ▶ Monitors
- ▶ Ada synchronization constructs
- ▶ Semaphores, P and V operations
- ▶ Blocking
- ▶ Spin locks
- ▶ I/O and data communication
- ▶ Interprocess communication

  ▶ Network Communication

  > Name

  > Address

  > Route

7. Naming and addressing

  ▶ Models, distributed

  ▶ Types

  ▶ Scope

  > Space scope

  > Extent (time scope)

  ▶ Aliasing

  ▶ Protection and authentication

References:

  ▶ C.G. Bell and J.C. Mudge, "The Evolution of the PDP-11"; Chapter 16 of C.G. Bell, J.C. Mudge, and J.E. McNamara, *Computer Engineering: A DEC View of Hardware Systems Design* [8].

  ▶ M. Ben-Ari, *Principles of Concurrent Programming* [9].

  ▶ E.W. Dijkstra, *Cooperating Sequential Processes* [30].

  ▶ A.N. Habermann, *Introduction to Operating System Design* [46].

  ▶ C.A.R. Hoare, *Communicating Sequential Processes* [51].

  ▶ R.C. Holt, G.S. Graham, E.D. Lazowska, and M.A. Scott, *Structured Concurrent Programming with Operating System Applications* [52].

  ▶ C. Seitz, *System Timing*; Chapter 7 of C. Mead and L. Conway, *Introduction to VLSI Systems* [77].

  ▶ R. Milner, *Communicating Systems* [78].

  ▶ A. Tanenbaum, *Computer Networks* [111].

Resource Requirements (software):

  ▶ operating system components for software laboratory: schedulers, storage allocators, etc.

  ▶ Driver and simulated load and timing apparatus

Implementation Considerations and Concerns:

  ▶ The best presentation of the material in this course depends on a careful balance between hardware, software, and theoretical issues. This requires a great deal of breadth from the instructor, something that may be difficult to find.

11.2.6. Program Organizations [313]

Prerequisites: FUNDAMENTAL STRUCTURES OF COMPUTER SCIENCE II [212]

Description: This course covers a variety of common program organizations and program development techniques that should be in the vocabulary of a competent software engineer. The student learns advanced methods for programming-in-the-small including implementation of modules to given specifications and some common program organizations. The course also covers techniques for reusing previous work (e.g.,program transformation techniques and generic definitions) and elementary design and specification.

Rationale: In previous courses, students have studied data structures, some programming languages, and some particular ways to organize and develop programs by putting individual statements together to make procedures. In software engineering courses they will study ways to put modules together to form systems. This course fills in the middle ground by presenting a variety of ways to put code fragments together to make modules. Consequently, the course presents a methodology for medium-scale program development and lays a foundation for SOFTWARE ENGINEERING [413]. In the same way that FUNDAMENTAL STRUCTURES OF COMPUTER SCIENCE II [212] and ALGORITHMS AND PROGRAMS [330] teach comparative data structures and LANGUAGES, INTERFACES, AND THEIR PROCESSORS [320] teaches comparative programming languages, this course teaches comparative program organizations—the program skeletons that good programmers carry in their heads.

Objectives: At the end of this course, a student will be able to:

- ► Select an appropriate program organization for a problem of moderate size (5-10 pages) and implement a program competently
- ► Use pre-existing definitions and development tools to expedite the development of such programs
- ► Implement a module to a given specification

Ideas: This course will be the primary carrier of the following:

- ► Standard program organizations
- ► Program development methodology for medium-scale programs
- ► Systematic methods for creating and connecting software components

It will reinforce or share responsibility for:

- ► Understanding that programs can be constructed or modified by other programs
- ► Engineering concerns in software construction

Topic Outline:

1. Ideas

- ▶ Notion of a program organization paradigm
- ▶ Advanced programming techniques and methodology
- ▶ Devising and evaluating alternative implementations
- ▶ Creating software by modifying software (when large-grain transformations emerge, they go here)
- ▶ Engineering concerns: reliability, reasoning about correctness and efficiency, informed selection among alternative implementations

2. Program organizations; examples drawn from:

- ▶ Abstract data types (use for connection to FUNDAMENTAL STRUCTURES OF COMPUTER SCIENCE II [212])
- ▶ Pipes/filters
- ▶ Table-driven interpreters
- ▶ Pattern-matching systems; production systems
- ▶ State machines
- ▶ Command-language processors (e.g. editors)
- ▶ Constraint systems
- ▶ Cooperating concurrent processes
- ▶ Object-oriented programming (message-passing systems)

3. Methodology

- ▶ Evaluation and selection of implementation alternatives
- ▶ Specification (formal and informal)
- ▶ Generic definitions and macros
- ▶ Transformation systems
- ▶ Reusable software
- ▶ Program development systems

References:

- ▶ O.J. Dahl, E.W. Dijkstra, and C.A.R. Hoare, *Structured Programming* [27].
- ▶ D. Gries, *The Science of Programming* [44].
- ▶ P. Hibbard, A. Hisgen, J. Rosenberg, M. Shaw, and M. Sherman, *Studies in Ada Style* [49].
- ▶ B.W. Kernighan and P.J. Plauger *Software Tools in Pascal* [59].

Resource Requirements (software):

- ▶ Templates and worked-out examples of the various program organizations included in the course.
- ▶ A software development environment to make assignment of large programs feasible.

► If case studies are used, the software being studied should be available for modification or measurement.

Implementation Considerations and Concerns:

► For the time being, this should be a lab course. It might, for example, be organized as a set of case studies, much in the style of data structure courses, with sample program organizations from the list above, abstract specifications and implementation alternatives for each, and evaluations of the result. As the formal theories that support these organizations grow, it should become more of a lecture course.

► The course should cover cases in both Pascal and LISP, one other programming language might be introduced.

11.2.7. Languages, Interfaces, and their Processors [320]

Prerequisites: FUNDAMENTAL STRUCTURES OF COMPUTER SCIENCE II [212]
REAL AND ABSTRACT MACHINES [240]

Description: This course examines the nature of programming languages and the programs that implement them. It covers the basic elements of programming language organization and implementation; it also touches on the design of interactive interfaces. The emphasis is on the elements of general-purpose programming languages that are common to many programming languages and on ideas that are also applicable to specialized systems. Implementation techniques covered include lexical analysis, simple parsing, semantic analysis including symbol tables and types, and interpretation for elementary arithmetic expressions. Programming projects include a simple interpreter and an interactive program.

Rationale: The traditional courses on programming languages are a "comparative languages" course and a "compiler" course; the compiler course also served as an example of a medium-sized system with a well-understood structure. Usually, however, the more fundamental objectives of understanding languages and system organization get lost in the press of, for example, learning three new programming languages or constructing a complete compiler for an Algol-class language. In addition, these courses omit a number of topics that are now of increasing importance to computer science. Such topics include the use of coherent systems of software development tools, human factors considerations for interfaces, engineering considerations concerning usability and reliability, and improved theoretical approaches to specifications of computations and policies. In addition, there has been a shift in the needs of the students: an increasing number of them end up creating programs to be used by laymen rather than modules that will be incorporated in large software systems.

We propose a three-course sequence that substantially revises the previous pair of courses:

- ▶ LANGUAGES, INTERFACES, AND THEIR PROCESSORS [320] deals with the structure and organization of programming languages and with the interface between programs and people. Since it is intended for a wide spectrum of students, it emphasizes techniques applicable to specialized interfaces as well as to general-purpose languages.

- ▶ TRANSDUCERS OF PROGRAMS [420] centers on the notion that programs should be manipulated by other programs as well as by people. The major examples are drawn from compilers, but tools for constructing compilers and a variety of techniques for re-using code are explored. Examples include automatic parser generation, macro/generic definition expansion, test data generation, use of integrated editors and program development databases.

- ▸ ADVANCED PROGRAMMING LANGUAGES AND COMPILERS [421] is concerned with programming language topics of specialized interest. These include comparative study of programming languages, optimization techniques, and the interaction between language design and implementation.

This section describes the first course (320) of this programming language sequence. The theme of this course is the description of computations. These descriptions are used both by humans and by computers. They may be either static, as in a conventional programming language, or dynamic, as in an interactive interface. The course covers both notations and the software systems that process the notations. Notations of interest include programming languages, specification formalisms, software interfaces such as command languages, and interactive systems such as graphics processors. Students are assumed to enter knowing Pascal and LISP plus several specialized systems such as operating system command languages, editors, text formatters, and electronic message systems, so there is a base of common experience to provide examples.

Specialized languages and packages account for an increasing share of modern software. They are especially important to naive users, who may use general-purpose languages rarely or not at all. As a result, there is a premium on good design and reliable implementation of these specialized systems. Design and implementation techniques developed for general-purpose programming languages apply as well to the specialized ones; the transfer is not, however, so obvious that students will make it without help. We believe that the changing style of computing justifies a shift in emphasis in the courses. Further, a shift to smaller languages will provide a large set of examples whose size is more manageable than many of the examples now used in compiler courses. The emergence of software development tools for constructing parts of language-like systems is also an advantage.

Objectives: At the end of this course, a student will be able to:

- ▸ Learn new programming languages or system interfaces with reasonable investment of effort
- ▸ Design and implement usable, reliable interfaces for small systems such as editors or data-management programs
- ▸ Evaluate language or interface designs
- ▸ Make competent use of the programming languages and systems taught in the course

Ideas: This course will be the primary carrier of the following:

- ► General structure and organization of programming languages
- ► Criteria for evaluating languages, including human factors concerns
- ► Implementation: data structures and algorithms for lexical analysis, symbol tables, and simple parsing

It will reinforce or share responsibility for:

- ► Abstraction methodologies
- ► Change of representation as a general tool for computer science
- ► The impact of notations on approaches to problems
- ► Introduction to several general-purpose languages of rather different character (Snobol, APL, etc)

Topic Outline:

This course includes a comparison of several general-purpose languages, the general principles of language and interface design, evaluation criteria and human factors concerns. The topics fall generally into three parts: The nature of general-purpose programming languages, the linguistic character of interfaces for command languages and many applications, and implementation techniques suitable for systems of the first two classes.

1. **Introduction to the theory of programming languages**

   - ► Note that at this level (sophomore/junior), one enumerates the design alternatives rather than expecting the comparison and evaluation to really sink in. In a certain sense, this is elementary anatomy; comparative anatomy comes in ADVANCED PROGRAMMING LANGUAGES AND COMPILERS [421], and genuine depth in language design is a graduate issue.

   - ► Structure of algorithmic languages

     - > Simple statements: statement sequencing; iteration and recursion; conditionals
     - > Data structures and declarations
     - > Addressing mechanisms (virtual addresses, indirection): variables, names vs. values, scope, binding, extent; storage allocation—implicit and explicit, structure and management   Types (and what is typed: values, variables,...); abstract data types
     - > Abstraction mechanisms: functions, procedures, and exception handlers

   - ► Syntax vs. semantics vs. pragmatics
   - ► Language as a communication/interface medium
   - ► Language (notation) as a means of shaping ideas
   - ► Techniques for defining programming languages (review of FUNDAMENTAL STRUCTURES OF COMPUTER SCIENCE I [211])

     - > Regular expressions for lexical structure
     - > BNF for syntax
     - > Existence of formal semantics methods

2. **Introduction to a third programming language**

   ▶ This language should be fairly different from Pascal and LISP

   ▶ Teach a characteristic core subset in a week

   ▶ The lectures on the nature of programming languages should overlap with actually learning the language (1-2 weeks)

3. **Evaluation criteria for languages**

   ▶ Simplicity, orthogonality, appropriateness, abstraction, etc

   ▶ Language complexity vs. implementation complexity

   ▶ Human factors—emphasis on the sorts of interfaces students use and create, not just on programming languages. This means graphics and human factors, among other things.

4. **Effect of programming language on program organization**

   ▶ Structured programming

   ▶ Recursion and list structures

   ▶ Applicative programming

   ▶ Shifting program organization paradigms with shift in language

5. **Interactive program organization**

   ▶ Screen handling

   ▶ Feedback during input, e.g., command completion and default generation

   ▶ Simple 2-dimensional interface design

6. **Special-purpose languages as languages**

   ▶ Compare structure (control, data, etc) with general-purpose languages.

   ▶ Relation between complexity of language and implementation, ease of use

   ▶ Examples, from: spreadsheet program, robot control language, word/text processing language, database query language, editor, etc

7. **Project:** build an interpreter with full-screen display, or an interface for a client application provided by the instructor. Study implementation techniques while students work on project.

8. **Processors and implementation techniques (survey)**

   ▶ Overview

      > Compilers, interpreters, linkers

      > Lexical analysis, parsing, symbol tables

      > Expression evaluation

      > Code generation; role of optimization

      > Macro processors, pseudo-operations, cross-references, other good assembler techniques

   ▶ Run-time representations, structures, and types

      > Display management

      > Storage management, including reference counts and garbage collection

9. Specific implementation techniques

- ► These are selected because of their applicability outside the world of compilers for general-purpose languages.
- ► Level of aspiration is complete treatment of regular languages plus the interpretation of arithmetic expressions as a special case of context-free.
- ► Lexical analysis and BNF (review of FUNDAMENTAL STRUCTURES OF COMPUTER SCIENCE I [211])
- ► Parser (generated with a tool)
- ► Elementary semantic analysis (symbol table, types on nodes of parse tree)

References:

- ► A.V. Ahō and J.D. Ullman, *Principles of Compiler Design* [5]. (The "Dragon Book")
- ► R.E. Griswold and M.T. Griswold, *A Snobol Primer* [45].
- ► H. Ledgard and M. Marcotty, *The Programming Language Landscape* [68].
- ► B.J. MacLennan, *Principles of Programming Languages: Design, Evaluation, and Implementation* [74].
- ► J.E. Nicholls, *The Structure and Design of Programming Languages* [83].
- ► S. Pakin, *APL\360 Reference Manual* [86].
- ► T.W. Pratt, *Programming Languages: Design and Implementation* [93].
- ► R.D. Tennent, *Principles of Programming Languages* [113].
- ► N. Wirth, *Algorithms + Data Structures = Programs* [125]. (especially Chapter 5)
- ► Texts on command languages, human engineering, and interactive systems

Resource Requirements (software):

- ► Sample systems
- ► Compiler-construction tools for lexical analysis and for simple syntactic and semantic analysis.
- ► Compiler lab: modules for lexer, symbol table, ... that can be composed to make a complete compiler. Ditto for components of an interpreter. These facilities are more important for TRANSDUCERS OF PROGRAMS [420], but they could be used here as well.

Implementation Considerations and Concerns:

- ► It is very hard to generalize about languages without at least 3 in

hand.   Pascal and LISP come from the prerequisite of
FUNDAMENTAL STRUCTURES OF COMPUTER SCIENCE II [212]; an
assembler comes from REAL AND ABSTRACT MACHINES [240].
Students should already know several special-purpose languages,
such as the operating system command language, the editor, the
text formatter, the mailer. Examples should draw heavily on these.
If time permits, another interactive spreadsheet system could be
taught.

▸ In addition, REAL AND ABSTRACT MACHINES [240] is a prerequisite
in order to ensure that students can appreciate the language-as-
abstract-machine viewpoint and to provide a feeling for the role of
the representation shift between a high-level language and a
machine language.

▸ The emergence of program development tools affects us in two
ways: first, they allow for larger, more realistic examples and
introduce students to the tools of the real world; second, they make
it possible to use the effects of the tools in the first course and defer
the mechanism (e.g., parsing) to a later course.

▸ Balance should be 50% what a language is, 50% broadly useful
implementations.

▸ See notes in topic outline

11.2.8. Algorithms and Programs [330]

Prerequisites: FUNDAMENTAL STRUCTURES OF COMPUTER SCIENCE II [212]

Description: An introduction to abstract algorithms and to their design, analysis, and realization. The goal of the course is to develop skill with practical algorithm design and analysis techniques and to develop the ability to apply these techniques to the construction of real systems.

Rationale: The treatment of algorithms begins in FUNDAMENTAL STRUCTURES OF COMPUTER SCIENCE II [212] with the algorithms that manipulate data structures; it continues through ALGORITHMS AND PROGRAMS [330] with a pragmatic view of the application of algorithmic ideas to reals systems and concludes with an abstract treatment of algorithms in ADVANCED ALGORITHMS [430]. This sequence provides a solid grounding in algorithm design and analysis.

In ALGORITHMS AND PROGRAMS [330] the student is presented with a collection of useful algorithms and with design and analysis techniques. The context is realistic enough to require meaningful choices about the application of these techniques. The point of view here is that algorithms (the abstractions) provide models that can be imposed on nasty real problems. Like all models, they do not match the real problems exactly, and some skill is required to use them well. Students need to learn a number of these models to use as tools; they also need practice in applying them to real problems.

Course ADVANCED ALGORITHMS [430], on the other hand, takes a more abstract view; it is directed towards teaching the fundamental ideas of problem diagnosis and algorithm design. This division of responsibilities is intended to provide all students with good problem solving skills for concrete algorithmic problems and to enable interested students to pursue topics in abstract algorithms in substantial depth.

Objectives: At the end of this course, a student will be able to

- Choose algorithms appropriate for many common computational problems.
- Analyze the use of computational resources by programs.
- Exploit constraints and structure to design good algorithms.
- Apply algorithmic ideas to write fast programs.
- Select appropriate tradeoffs for speed, space, and reliability.

Ideas: This course will be the primary carrier of the following:

- Algorithm design principles
- Analysis techniques for algorithms
- Pertinence of abstract algorithms to program construction

Topic Outline:

1. **Data structures and algorithms** (review of FUNDAMENTAL STRUCTURES OF COMPUTER SCIENCE II [212])

   ▶ Queues, stacks, graphs, heaps, balanced binary trees, priority queues

2. **Analysis of algorithms**

   ▶ What to analyze

   ▶ Order arithmetic

   ▶ Software timing and monitoring tools

3. **Problem assessment and algorithm design techniques**

   ▶ Weak methods: local search, heuristic search, evaluation functions

   ▶ Exploiting structure

   ▶ Constraints

   ▶ Problem reformulation: time vs. space, precomputation, dynamic data updating

   ▶ Search: connected components, shortest paths

   ▶ Divide-and-Conquer: binary search, sorting, selection

   ▶ Greedy Method: Dijkstra's algorithm, spanning trees

   ▶ Dynamic Programming: path algorithms, traveling salesman

   ▶ Probabilistic algorithms

4. **Implementation considerations**

   ▶ Choosing representations

   ▶ Pragmatic constraints: speed vs. maintainability

   ▶ Improving performance: bottlenecks, profiling, gross estimates

5. **NP-completeness**

   ▶ Satisfiability, clique, Hamiltonian circuits, etc.

6. **Particular algorithms; examples will be selected from the following classes:**

   ▶ Mathematical algorithms: arithmetic, random numbers, polynomials, Gaussian elimination, curve fitting, integration

   ▶ Sorting: elementary sorting methods, Quicksort, radix sorting, priority queues, selection and merging, external sorting

   ▶ Searching: elementary searching methods, balanced trees, hashing, radix searching, external searching

   ▶ String processing: string searching, pattern matching, parsing, file compression, cryptology

   ▶ Geometric algorithms: elementary geometric methods, finding the convex hull, range searching, geometric intersection, closest point problems

   ▶ Graph algorithms: elementary graph algorithms, connectivity, weighted graphs, directed graphs, network flow, matching

7. **Advanced topics: a selection from**

   ▶ Algorithm machines: general approaches, perfect shuffles, systolic arrays

- ► The Fast Fourier Transform: evaluate, multiply, interpolate, complex roots of unity, evaluation and interpolation at the roots of unity, implementation
- ► Dynamic Programming: knapsack problem, matrix chain product, optimal binary search trees, shortest paths, time and space requirements
- ► Linear programming: linear programs, geometric interpretation, the simplex method, implementation
- ► Parallel algorithms: sorting, searching, in parallel
- ► Exhaustive search: exhaustive search in graphs, backtracking, permutation generation, approximation algorithms
- ► NP-complete problems: deterministic and nondeterministic polynomial-time algorithms, NP-completeness, Cook's theorem, some NP-complete problems

References:

- ► A.V. Aho, J.D. Hopcroft, and J.E. Ullman, *The Design and Analysis of Computer Algorithms* [4].
- ► A.V. Aho, J.D. Hopcroft, and J.E. Ullman, *Data Structures and Algorithms* [6].
- ► J.L. Bentley, *Writing Efficient Programs* [10].
- ► J.L. Bentley, *Programming Pearls* [11].
- ► D. Gries, *The Science of Programming* [44].
- ► D.E. Knuth, *The Art of Computer Programming* [60, 61, 64].
- ► B. Lampson, *Notes on System Design* [66].
- ► E.M. Reingold, J. Nievergelt, and N. Deo, *Combinatorial Algorithms* [96].
- ► R. Sedgewick, *Algorithms* [102].

Resource Requirements (software):

- ► Library of data types and implementations
- ► Test bed for timing and program development
- ► Timing support
- ► Sample data sets

Implementation Considerations and Concerns:

- ► This course would be required for a major because, of all the 300-level courses, it most clearly captures the interplay of theoretical ideas with practical programming problems. Since so many traditional algorithms courses already exist, there will be a tendency for this course to drift toward those models. It is important to resist that drift.
- ► The algorithms listed in the outline are presented as a menu of examples. It is not possible to cover them all in one course, and the

integrative material should not be slighted in favor of a few extra algorithms.

▸ Some algorithms may be covered in other courses such as numerical linear algebra or graph theory.

11.2.9. Formal Languages, Automata, and Complexity [350]

Prerequisites: FUNDAMENTAL STRUCTURES OF COMPUTER SCIENCE I [211]

Description: This course introduces the basic ideas of formal languages, computability and complexity theory.   It contains only the more fundamental material on complexity, to give the student an overall feel for the topic; the more advanced aspects are covered in an advanced course COMPLEXITY THEORY [451]. Some introductory material will be assumed from the pre-requisite course FUNDAMENTAL STRUCTURES OF COMPUTER SCIENCE I [211].

This course begins with an introduction to finite state automata and their relationship to classes of formal languages. A finite automaton is a mathematical model of a finite-state system; computer science has many examples of finite state systems. Formal languages are of great importance, notably in defining programming languages and in formalizing the notion of parsing. The material of this course is primarily concerned with the relationship between the various classes of language and various types of automaton. Thus it is shown that particular classes of automata recognize particular types of formal language. Since this is a first course dealing in detail with these concepts, it is important to emphasize these ideas in a strongly applied context, to bring out the connections with areas such as software support (parsers for programming languages, simulators for automata, for example).

Computability is concerned with characterizing the class of problems that can be solved, in a well defined sense, by a computer. In complexity theory the interest lies in how much space or how much time is required to solve a problem (relative to the size of the problem); the recognition problem for various formal languages serves to provide examples of problems of various degrees of complexity. Again, it is important to emphasize the practical applications of the results.

Rationale: Automata and the related notion of computability by an automaton are fundamental to many branches of computer science. Likewise, formal languages underpin much work on parsing, programming language theory and practice. This course can be organized around the theme of formal languages, their generation by grammars and their recognition by finite state machines.   Problems associated with formal languages, such as ambiguity, can be used to illustrate the notions of decidability and undecidability; the various recognition problems for languages serve to illustrate the problems of various degrees of complexity.

Objectives: At the end of this course, a student will have a feeling for the theoretical limitations of computers, and how restrictions on working space and running time affect the capability of computers to solve problems. He will have an idea of how formal languages are used in

theory and in practice. This will help in later courses such as ADVANCED
PROGRAMMING LANGUAGES AND COMPILERS [421].

Ideas: This course will be the primary carrier of the following:

- Formal languages
- Automata of various kinds
- Equivalences between machines and corresponding languages
- Impact of notation on the way we think
- Recognition and generation problems
- Computability by abstract devices
- Elementary aspects of complexity theory

It will reinforce or share responsibility for:

- Computability and decidability
- Inductive definitions and inductive arguments

Topic Outline:

1. **Regular languages and finite-state automata:**

   - Recognition of a language by an automaton
   - Regular sets as the languages recognized by finite automata
   - Regular expressions, finite automata
   - Equivalence of deterministic and nondeterministic finite automata
   - Minimization of a finite automaton
   - Algorithm for equivalence of finite automata (decidable problem)
   - The Pumping lemma and its use in proving non-regularity
   - Closure properties of regular sets
   - Algebraic characterization of regular sets
   - Myhill-Nerode theorem and its uses

2. **Context-free languages as the languages recognized by pushdown automata**

   - Context-free grammars, pushdown automata
   - Examples of CFLs which are not regular
   - Undecidability of equivalence problem for CFLs
   - Undecidability of ambiguity problem for CFLs
   - Closure properties of CFLs
   - Properties of grammars: emptiness, ambiguity, LL, LR

3. **Computability**

   - Algorithms: intuitive notion of algorithm as effective procedure
   - Formalization of the notion of algorithm
   - Turing machines.
   - Register machines

- ▶ Computable functions, sets
- ▶ Computable by Turing machine iff computable by register machine
- ▶ Church's thesis

4. Recursive function theory

- ▶ Recursive functions and sets
- ▶ Recursively enumerable sets

5. Decidable and undecidable problems

- ▶ Halting problem
- ▶ Post correspondence problem
- ▶ Rice's theorem
- ▶ Reduction of a problem to an undecidable problem to show undecidability
- ▶ Diagonal arguments
- ▶ Examples drawn from context free languages (CFLs) (e.g., equivalence problem for CFLs and ambiguity problem for CFLs)

6. Universality and recursion

- ▶ Godel numbering
- ▶ Universal Turing machines
- ▶ Kleene's T-predicate
- ▶ The s-m-n theorem
- ▶ The recursion theorems
- ▶ Use of universal machines (e.g., to show computability of Ackermann's function)

7. Complexity theory:

- ▶ Distinction between computability and complexity
- ▶ Space complexity
- ▶ Time complexity
- ▶ Complexity relative to deterministic and nondeterministic computation
- ▶ Survey of the time and space hierarchies: PTIME, NP, RPTIME, co-NP, PSPACE, etc.
- ▶ Cook's theorem
- ▶ Examples of problems known to lie in each hierarchical level: graph isomorphism, recognition problems

References:

- ▶ N.J. Cutland, *Computability: An Introduction to Recursive Function Theory* [26].
- ▶ J.E. Hopcroft and J.D. Ullman, *Introduction to Automata Theory, Languages and Computation* [53].
- ▶ H.R. Lewis and C.H. Papadimitriou, *Elements of the Theory of Computation* [70].

- M. Minsky, *Computation: Finite and Infinite Machines* [79].
- H. Rogers, *Theory of Recursive Functions and Effective Computability* [98].

Resource Requirements:

- Grammar support tools: parser generators for various classes of grammars, drivers for testing grammars

Implementation Considerations and Concerns:

- The outline contains a lot of material, possibly too much for a one-semester course. It may be necessary to extract the more advanced material on computability and design an advanced course covering this, leaving only the basic material on computability here in FORMAL LANGUAGES, AUTOMATA, AND COMPLEXITY [350].

11.2.10. Logic for Computer Science [351]

Prerequisites: FUNDAMENTAL STRUCTURES OF COMPUTER SCIENCE I [211]
One 300-level math or theoretical computer science course

Description: The basic results and techniques of logic are presented and related to fundamental issues in computer science.

Rationale: Logic provides essential foundations for our activity in computer science. It teaches us to distinguish between abstraction and realization and, in particular, between language and meaning. Programming languages are formal languages; the techniques we use to give them meaning and to reason about them find their foundations in logic. Logic also teaches us how to reason about the world by manipulating symbols; this is directly analogous to the activity of computation. Finally, the basic results of logic reveal the inherent limitations on our activity of formal reasoning.

Objectives: At the end of this course, a student will be able to:

- ▸ Understand the role of formalization and formal reasoning in computer science.
- ▸ Be familiar with the basic techniques and results of mathematical logic.

Ideas: This course will be the primary carrier of the following:

- ▸ Fundamental concepts and results from logic
- ▸ The notion of formal reasoning

It will reinforce or share responsibility for:

- ▸ Syntax and semantics
- ▸ Computability
- ▸ Reasoning about programs

Topic Outline:

1. **Syntactical structures and computability**
   - ▸ Lists and functions—The basis for a simple model of computation
   - ▸ An analysis of the notion of computation
   - ▸ Syntactic structures in logic and programming

2. **Formal reasoning**
   - ▸ Examples of formal deductive systems
     - > Natural deduction
     - > Hoare's logic

   - ▸ Propositional and predicate calculus
   - ▸ The formalization of mathematical reasoning
     - > Reasoning about programs

3. Semantics and completeness

▶ Structures and truth

▶ Completeness of first-order logic

▶ Church's thesis revisited

▶ Semantics and reasoning about programs

4. Incompleteness and undecidability

▶ Decidability and undecidability

▶ Presburger arithmetic

▶ The incompleteness of first-order number theory

References:

▶ G.S. Boolos and R.C. Jeffrey, *Computability and Logic* [15].

▶ H. Enderton, *A Mathematical Introduction to Logic* [34].

▶ D. van Dalen, *Logic and Structure* [120].

11.2.11. Introduction to Artificial Intelligence [360]

Prerequisites: FUNDAMENTAL STRUCTURES OF COMPUTER SCIENCE II [212]
or INFORMATION PROCESSING PSYCHOLOGY AND AI [PSY 213]

Description: This course teaches the fundamentals of artificial intelligence, including problem solving techniques, search, heuristic methods, and knowledge representation. Ideas are illustrated by sample programs and systems drawn from various branches of AI. Small programming projects will also be used to convey the central ideas of the course.

Rationale: This course provides a jumping off point for students in ARTIFICIAL INTELLIGENCE—COGNITIVE PROCESSES [460] and ARTIFICIAL INTELLIGENCE—ROBOTICS [461]. It provides students with an overview of the field without requiring the mathematics background used in the Robotics courses or the psychological emphasis used in the Cognitive Processes course.

Objectives: At the end of this course, a student will be able to

- Program large systems in Lisp
- Use AI techniques to solve difficult problems
- Read and understand the artificial intelligence (AI) literature

Ideas: This course will be the primary carrier of the following:

- Advanced Lisp techniques
- Weak methods and problem solving
- Knowledge representation and inference
- Introduction to expert systems and natural language processing.

It will reinforce or share responsibility for:

- Lisp programming beyond the level of FUNDAMENTAL STRUCTURES OF COMPUTER SCIENCE II [212]
- Production systems and embedded languages (also covered in PROGRAM ORGANIZATIONS [313] and LANGUAGES, INTERFACES, AND THEIR PROCESSORS [320])
- Knowledge representation (also covered in BIG DATA [410] and ARTIFICIAL INTELLIGENCE—COGNITIVE PROCESSES [460])
- Search (also covered in ALGORITHMS AND PROGRAMS [330])

Topic Outline:

1. Introduction
   - History
   - What is AI?
   - Intellectual issues

2. **Problem solving**
   - ▶ Problem spaces
   - ▶ Heuristic search

3. **Search methods**
   - ▶ Hillclimbing
   - ▶ Depth-first
   - ▶ Breadth-first
   - ▶ Best-first
   - ▶ Exploiting constraints
   - ▶ Dependency-directed backtracking
   - ▶ Means-ends analysis
   - ▶ Mini-max
   - ▶ Alpha-beta

4. **Planning**
   - ▶ Strips
   - ▶ Build
   - ▶ Abstrips

5. **Knowledge representation**
   - ▶ Logic and resolution
   - ▶ Default reasoning
   - ▶ Semantic nets
   - ▶ Parallel implementations of semantic nets
   - ▶ Frames

6. **Natural languages**
   - ▶ ATN's
   - ▶ Semantic grammars
   - ▶ Conceptual dependency
   - ▶ Scripts

7. **Production systems**
   - ▶ Varieties of production system
   - ▶ Use as psychological models
   - ▶ Use in expert systems

8. **Learning**
   - ▶ Learning concepts and laws from examples
   - ▶ Learning when to apply productions
   - ▶ Learning new productions from old
   - ▶ Discovering new concepts
   - ▶ Learning in parallel networks

9. The future of AI

- ▶ Application areas
- ▶ Moral issues
- ▶ Relation to human cognition

References:

- ▶ E. Rich, *Artificial Intelligence* [97]
- ▶ P.H. Winston, *Artificial Intelligence* [124]
- ▶ P.H. Winston and B.K.P. Horn, *LISP* [123]

Resource Requirements:

- ▶ Copies of the example programs (Eliza, Mycin, *etc.*)
- ▶ Lisp programming environment
- ▶ Lisp cycles
- ▶ Lisp cycles
- ▶ Lisp cycles

Implementation Considerations and Concerns:

- ▶ The instructor has a responsibility to provide a *broad* overview of AI and a solid foundation in Lisp, Knowledge representation, and problem solving techniques.
- ▶ Lisp coverage in FUNDAMENTAL STRUCTURES OF COMPUTER SCIENCE II [212] may be spotty, and review might be necessary.

11.2.12. Introduction to Robotics [361]

Prerequisites: FUNDAMENTAL STRUCTURES OF COMPUTER SCIENCE II [212]
> **plus**   LINEAR ALGEBRA [MATH 341]
> METHODS OF APPLIED MATHEMATICS I [MATH 259]
> CALCULUS II (MULTIVARIATE CALCULUS) [MATH 122]
> **or** equivalent background in mathematics and physics

Description: This course covers intelligence systems which deal in some way with the physical world, either through visual, acoustic, or tactile means. Topics include vision, speech recognition, manipulation, and locomotion.

Rationale: This is a sister course to INTRODUCTION TO ARTIFICIAL INTELLIGENCE [360].   It provides basic knowledge for ARTIFICIAL INTELLIGENCE—ROBOTICS [461].   By making INTRODUCTION TO ROBOTICS [361] a separate course from INTRODUCTION TO ARTIFICIAL INTELLIGENCE [360], it is possible to ensure that students have sufficient mathematical background for them to understand intelligent robotics systems. It is also desirable that students entering this course have a basic grounding in AI (which may not help directly in this course, but does provide a context).

Objectives: At the end of this course, a student will be able to:

> ► Understand the fundamental approaches used in intelligent robotic systems.

> ► Read and understand literature on vision, speech, and manipulation.

Ideas: This course will be the primary carrier of the following:

> ► Perception (vision and speech)

> ► Three dimensional modelling

> ► Control of physical systems

Topic Outline:

1. **Vision**

> ► Early image processing (Edge and region extraction)

> ► Images and shapes (line drawing understanding, shape from methods)

> ► Motion understanding from images

> ► Shape representation

> ► Model-based vision systems

2. **Speech recognition**

> ► Signal processing

> ► Feature extraction

> ► Recognition systems (Isolated word recognition, Continuous speech recognition)

3. Manipulation and locomotion

- ▶ Kinematics and dynamics
- ▶ Trajectory and task planning
- ▶ Control
- ▶ Robot programming
- ▶ Locomotion (gait analysis and dynamic balance)

References:

- ▶ D. Ballard and C. Brown, *Computer Vision* [7].
- ▶ Brady et al., *Robot Motion*, [16].
- ▶ R. Paul, *Robot Manipulators: Mathematics, Programming, and Control* [89].

Resource requirements:

- ▶ This course needs at least some if not all of the resources specified for the follow-up course, ARTIFICIAL INTELLIGENCE—ROBOTICS [461].
- ▶ The most important resources are hardware and software for manipulating images
- ▶ Robot manipulators (or software simulators) are also very important

Implementation Considerations and Concerns:

- ▶ This course is a part of the Artificial Intelligence group, and must be taught in such a way that it does not become a course in "Robot Engineering" or "Robot Math".
- ▶ We would have preferred to organize this course by technique and method, rather than by application, but were unable to find a satisfactory organization.
- ▶ The actual prerequisite courses in mathematics and physics can be rather flexible, so long as the necessary mathematical skills are acquired. However, in order for the prerequisites to be flexible in practice, a good description of the necessary skills is required.

11.3. Advanced Computer Science Courses

These courses are of specialized interest to computer scientists. They are suitable for a Master's program as well as for advanced students in a Bachelor's program.

In addition to the courses we define here, some of the content of computer science as described in Chapter 5 may be taught in departments other than computer science. These departments include mathematics, electrical engineering, psychology, and others. We have generally avoided designing courses that cover material taught at Carnegie-Mellon in these other departments.

To show more complete coverage of computer science, however, we list here the titles of courses that should be jointly listed by computer science and another department. Catalog descriptions for these courses appear in Chapter 12.

▶ MODERN ALGEBRA [MATH 473 / CS 452]

▶ LARGE-SCALE SCIENTIFIC COMPUTING [MATH 712 / CS 453]

Some of the courses outlined in this section may also be jointly listed. In particular, COMPUTER ARCHITECTURE [440] can be listed in the Electrical Engineering Department, ADVANCED ALGORITHMS [430] resembles APPLIED GRAPH THEORY [MATH 484], and COMPLEXITY THEORY [451] resembles THEORY OF ALGORITHMS [MATH 451].

11.3.1. Independent Project [400]

Prerequisites: FUNDAMENTAL STRUCTURES OF COMPUTER SCIENCE II [212]
Two more courses (beyond 212) with Bs or better
Instructor's permission, based on acceptance of proposal

Description: This is an independent project laboratory for the most advanced students. The student will design and construct a substantial software or hardware system under the supervision of a member of the faculty. Before construction of the project may proceed, a detailed design proposal must be submitted to and accepted by the faculty advisor. A design review with the advisor will be held at mid-term time. A final review of the functioning system and its supporting documentation will be held at the end of the semester. The intention is to permit the best students to exercise their design skills in the construction of a real system, so good design practice and good documentation are mandatory. The production of a functioning but undocumented system will not be sufficient. The instructor may accept projects intended to last two semesters in which case the review at the end of the first semester will be another major design review.

Rationale: Computer scientists going out to graduate school or to the practice of programming need to be able to design and construct good systems. This requires an appreciation of the difficulties of building a production-quality system, difficulties that go beyond the scope of toy systems built as part of lower level courses. This course will provide the advanced student with the opportunity to design and build a significant piece of hardware or software on his own, with experienced system builders available as instructors and teaching assistants to consult, advise, and criticize.

Objectives: At the end of this course, a student will be able to:

▸ Design a real system

▸ Document a real system

▸ Construct a real system

Ideas: This course will be the primary carrier of the following:

▸ Independent formulation and execution of projects

It will reinforce or share responsibility for:

▸ Software design principles

▸ Hardware design principles

References: F. Brooks, *The Mythical Man-Month* [17]

Resource Requirements:

▸ A substantial host machine, plus access to others

▸ A well outfitted hardware/software lab

▸ A lab bench or suitable office space for each student

Implementation Considerations and Concerns:

▸ This course is intended to have serious intellectual content. It should not be permitted to deteriorate into a simple home for hacking.

▸ It is important that the students in this course have access to experienced system builders. The teaching of this course will be expensive in all domains, including people and inanimate resources. It would be better not to offer it than to reduce the quality.

▸ In the course as described, the students are independent of one another and may even involve different instructor/advisors. The course could also be organized around group projects, interdependent projects, or a single problem to be solved by all students.

11.3.2. Undergraduate Thesis [401]

Prerequisites: FUNDAMENTAL STRUCTURES OF COMPUTER SCIENCE II [212]
Two more courses (beyond 212) with B's or better
Instructor's permission, based on acceptance of proposal

Description: This is an independent study and research course for the most advanced students. The student will write an undergraduate thesis or carry out a program of directed reading. Objectives for the course of study will be established by the student and a faculty advisor. With agreement of a faculty advisor, an undergraduate thesis project may be planned for two semesters

Rationale: This course provides students with the opportunity to pursue in depth the study of a topic that is not part of the general curriculum. It is similar to INDEPENDENT PROJECT [400], but the end result is an expository document rather than a system. It is expected that the student will work closely with a faculty advisor.

Objectives: At the end of this course a student will be able to:

► Organize the description of a collection of scientific findings and report the result in an expository technical paper

► Use the library for background research

► Do independent research

Ideas: This course will be the primary carrier of the following:

► Independent formulation and execution of a planned program of study.

Resource requirements:

► A pool of faculty to supervise students

11.3.3. Research Seminar [409]

Prerequisites: FUNDAMENTAL STRUCTURES OF COMPUTER SCIENCE II [212]
> Two more courses (beyond 212) with Bs or better

Description: Students attend the regular research seminars of the Computer Science Department and submit short written summaries.

Rationale: The Computer Science Department conducts a rich and varied set of public seminar series throughout the academic year. Undergraduates with sufficient maturity and experience in the field can benefit from attending, even if they do not completely understand the material presented. Attending these seminars is a good way to learn about very current ideas and to appreciate the scope and excitement of the field.

Objectives: At the end of this course, a student will:

- ▸ Be acquainted with some of the new ideas in computer science.

- ▸ Be able to write a short summary of a presentation on a technical topic.

Topic Outline:

> Certain regular seminar series plus selected individual seminars will be approved for this course. Students select seminars to suit individual preferences. Each student should plan to attend an average of one seminar per week. After the seminar, the student prepares a one-page (250-500 word) summary and critical appraisal of the seminar in his or her own words. Ten of these summaries—from any combination of approved seminars—are required for completion of the course. An introduction to writing short technical summaries will be presented at the beginning of the course.

Resource Requirements:

- ▸ Doughnuts

Implementation Considerations and Concerns:

- ▸ This course requires an ongoing seminar series. Research seminars are fine; an undergraduate can get a sense of the nature of research and creativity without completely understanding the material.

- ▸ This course could carry about a third of the credit of a normal course. It is intended to require two to three hours per week.

- ▸ The summaries serve two functions. They provide practice in writing short summaries of scientific material, and they encourage the students to be active rather than passive listeners.

11.3.4. Big Data [410]

Prerequisites: TIME AND RESOURCES [310]
                LANGUAGES, INTERFACES, AND THEIR PROCESSORS [320]
                PROBABILITY AND APPLIED STATISTICS [STAT 211 / CS 250]

Description: The central theme of this course is the storage and
    manipulation of large amounts of data. Topics include user data models,
    underlying data storage techniques, data representations, algorithms for
    data retrieval, specialized data manipulation languages, and techniques
    for providing reliability and security. Systems that permit the storage and
    retrieval of large amounts of data are studied.

Rationale: Although the topics in this course could be distributed among an
    algorithms course (external data storage and data representations), an
    operating systems course (reliability and security techniques), and a
    language course (data manipulation languages and models), we have
    chosen to incorporate them into one course for three reasons: First, the
    central theme of all these topics is the storage and manipulation of large
    collections of data.   Second, the storage and manipulation of large
    quantities of data represents one of the major applications of computers.
    Third, a unified course on these topics provides an opportunity for
    students to focus on large systems and some well understood techniques
    for their organization.

Objectives: At the end of this course, a student will be able to:

  ▶ Understand the goals of systems that deal with large quantities of
    data

  ▶ Understand techniques for making reliable resources from
    unreliable ones

  ▶ Understand and apply security and protection principles

  ▶ Use certain example systems

  ▶ Understand some of the algorithms and data structures used to
    organize such systems

  ▶ Analyze and evaluate the performance of large resource
    management systems

Ideas: This course will be the primary carrier of the following:

  ▶ Multilevel naming

  ▶ Binding (e.g., of decisions as well as names)

  ▶ Security techniques

  ▶ Reliability techniques

  ▶ Algorithms and data structures for external data storage

It will reinforce or share responsibility for:

- ► Explaining the use of specialized high level languages
- ► Presenting layered abstractions
- ► Naming, binding, addressing

Topic Outline:

1. **Files and access methods**
   - ► Sorting and searching
     - > B-Trees
     - > Multi-level storage structures
     - > Memory hierarchy
     - > Hashing
     - > Multi-key organizations

   - ► Other aspects of file organization
     - > Physical allocation
     - > Organizations for availability
     - > Performance issues in file storage

2. **Classical database management:**
   - ► Modelling at User Level
     - > Utility of this level of abstraction
     - > Classical data models and languages
       - ≫ Relational
       - ≫ Hierarchical
       - ≫ Network

     - > Example models

   - ► Detailed study of relational model
     - > Example Language: SQL
     - > Embedding of SQL within procedural language
     - > Example SQL application

3. **Topics in the storage of data**
   - ► Naming
     - > Long life
     - > Secure
     - > Autonomous

   - ► Approaches to data integrity and reliability
     - > Atomicity
     - > Use of redundancy
     - > Old master/new master schemes

- ► Sharing/concurrent access: consistency
  - > Synchronization aspects
  - > Recovery considerations
  - > Role of transactions

- ► Security, privacy, and authentication
  - > Capabilities vs. authorization lists
  - > Access protection and file security
  - > Administrative concerns
  - > Role of encryption
    - ≫ Public key encryption
    - ≫ Private key encryption

- ► Analysis

4. Non-traditional databases

- ► Storage of "knowledge"
- ► Issues in knowledge representation
- ► Non-uniform data in databases

5. Emerging public information utilities

- ► Library search
- ► Electronic publishing
- ► Teletext-type systems
- ► Community bulletin boards

References:

- ► C.J. Date, *An Introduction to Database Systems, Volumes 1 and 2* [28, 29]
- ► J.D. Ullman, *Principles of Database Systems* [116].

Resource Requirements:

- ► One or more production-quality database systems for use and comparison.

Implementation Considerations and Concerns:

- ► The convenient textbooks are conventional database texts. The instructor should be sure to make the linkages to programming languages (naming issues), artificial intelligence (knowledge representation), computer systems (effect of hardware considerations on database design), and operating systems (concurrency, synchronization, distributed databases).

11.3.5. Communications and Networks [411]

Prerequisites: TIME AND RESOURCES [310]
       PROBABILITY AND APPLIED STATISTICS [STAT 211 / CS 250]

Description: This course is an introduction to network communication, from the physics governing the underlying mechanisms through high-level network protocols.

Rationale: In recent years the extensive interconnection of computer systems and the concomitant increase in sophistication of existing communication systems has begun to blur the distinction between computation and communication. This course is intended to provide computer scientists with an integrated understanding of the important ideas from information theory, operating systems, and computer architecture.

Objectives: At the end of this course, a student will be able to:

▶ Analyze the performance of a communication system

▶ Understand and explain network architecture issues

▶ Understand and analyze communication protocols

Ideas: This course will be the primary carrier of the following:

▶ Quantifiability of information

▶ Coding for error correction and for data compression

▶ Communication network architecture and protocols

This course will share responsibility for or reinforce the following:

▶ Distributed naming

▶ Concurrency and synchronization

Topic Outline:

1. Information and communication

   ▶ Signals, energy, and noise

   ▶ Channels

      > Source, destination

      > Alphabet

      > Noise and errors

      > SNR

   ▶ Information theory

      > Quantity of information: entropy

      > Shannon's theorem

   ▶ Coding

      > Error correcting codes

> Channel capacity

> Source encoding

> Rate distortion theory

2. Architecture

▶ Busses

▶ Local area networks

▶ Larger scale networks

3. Protocols

▶ Data link level

> Protocols: bit and byte oriented

▶ Local area networks

> Ring

> Contention

> Digital switch

▶ Network level

> Store and forward

> Virtual circuit

> Datagram

▶ Intermediate level

> Process-process

> Multiplexing

▶ Location-transparent interprocess communication (IPC)

> Messages

> Remote procedure call (RPC)

▶ Application level protocols

> Presentation

> Graphics

4. Policy issues

▶ Access

▶ Security

▶ Privacy

References:

▶ P. Green, *Computer Network Architectures and Protocols* [42]

▶ Pierce and Posner, *Introduction to Communication Science and Systems*, [90].

▶ A. Tanenbaum, *Computer Networks* [111].

Resource Requirements

► Code for some existing communication system to read (e.g. IP/TCP)

Implementation Considerations and Concerns:

► This could be either a heavily theoretical course or a very hands-on engineering oriented course. That decision might be up to the instructor doing the actual teaching.

11.3.6. Software Engineering [413]

Prerequisites: PROGRAM ORGANIZATIONS [313]
LANGUAGES, INTERFACES, AND THEIR PROCESSORS [320]

Description: The student studies the nature of the program development task when many people, many modules, many versions, or many years are involved in designing, developing, and maintaining the system. The issues are both technical (e.g., design, specification, version control) and administrative (e.g., cost estimation and elementary management). The course will consist primarily of working in small teams on the cooperative creation and modification of software systems.

Rationale: This course extends the advanced program structures course by broadening the scope of attention to large-scale systems. This yields a natural progression from individual elements (statements or data structures) in FUNDAMENTAL STRUCTURES OF COMPUTER SCIENCE I AND II [211/212] through module-sized elements in PROGRAM ORGANIZATIONS [313] to large systems. Analysis and evaluation techniques are included throughout, but the emphasis on estimation and overall efficiency is greatest here. In addition, issues of reliability, testing, and implementation and documentation of a substantial user interface will be addressed here.

Objectives: At the end of this course, a student will be able to:

  ▶ Understand the issues in large-scale software development

  ▶ Participate as a team member in such a development

  ▶ Write specifications for simple modules that will be combined with other modules

  ▶ Implement a program or module that satisfies such a specification

Ideas: This course will be the primary carrier of the following:

  ▶ Complexity of large-scale software and tools for dealing with it

  It will reinforce or share responsibility for:

  ▶ Significance of tools for developing software

Topic Outline:

1. Elementary management

2. Cost estimation (of routines and larger code units)

3. Multiple people, versions, years, modules, modifications

4. Advanced design and specification; decomposition into modules

5. Programming-in-the-large

6. Properties of systems

  ▶ Reliability

  ▶ Generality

- ► Efficiency
- ► Complexity
- ► Compatibility
- ► Modularity
- ► Sharing

7. **System design and development principles**
    - ► Design tradeoffs
    - ► Computer system reliability, speed, capacity, cost
    - ► Development methodologies and tools
    - ► Design automation
    - ► Program specification
    - ► Maintenance and release policy (test sites, etc.)
    - ► Rapid prototyping and partial evaluation
    - ► Protection and security
    - ► Resource allocation
    - ► System evaluation and development aids

8. **Modification, planning for modification**

9. **Making implementation meet specifications**

10. **Models and modelling**
    - ► System modelling (version control)
    - ► What models are and how to use/construct them
    - ► Empirical vs. analytic models
    - ► Validation
    - ► Specific models (at this level, introduction only)
        - > Queueing-theoretic models for operating systems and hardware
        - > Productivity and life-cycle models (esp. their limitations)

11. **Monitoring tools and techniques for improving efficiency**

12. **Human factors, user interfaces**

13. **Examples of systems**
    - ► Large software systems, some involving concurrency issues
    - ► Distributed systems
    - ► Compilers, operating systems
    - ► Batch vs. time-sharing systems
    - ► File management
    - ► System accounting
    - ► The multiprogramming executive (MPX) operating system
    - ► Process control

14. **Current state of the art: APSEs, Gandalf, etc**

15. **Software systems**
   - ▶ Systems and utility programs
   - ▶ System structure
   - ▶ Parallelism in operating systems
     - \> Mutual exclusion
     - \> Synchronization

16. **Programming style and techniques**
   - ▶ Table-driven schemes

17. **Management, societal, economic, and legal aspects**
   - ▶ Computing economics: acquisition and operation
   - ▶ Copyrights, licensing and patents, computer crime

18. **Documentation**

19. **Software systems**
   - ▶ Memory management
   - ▶ File systems
   - ▶ Directories
   - ▶ Backup and recovery
   - ▶ Permanent and transient data: caching, buffering, atomic transactions, stable storage
   - ▶ Redundancy, encoding, encryption
   - ▶ Database management systems (DBMS)

References:

- ▶ B. W. Boehm, *Software Engineering Economics* [13].
- ▶ F. Brooks, *The Mythical Man-Month* [17].
- ▶ G. Myers, *Software Reliability: Principles and Practices* [80].
- ▶ G. Myers, *Composite/Structured Design* [81].
- ▶ M. Shooman, *Software Engineering* [105]
- ▶ E. Yourdon and L.L. Constantine, *Structured Design* [128].
- ▶ M.V. Zelkowitz, A.C. Shaw, and J.D. Gannon, *Principles of Software Engineering and Design* [129].

Resource Requirements (software):

- ▶ A program development environment will be essential.

Implementation Considerations and Concerns:

- ▶ It is imperative that students actually use the *best available tools* for version control, text editing, etc. Students will invariably draw on their experiences in actual system development rather than on what they have read or heard in lectures.

- Since the majority of learning in this course is by doing, a traditional course format may not be best. The instructor should spend time counselling teams and walking them through code-reading sessions, etc., in addition to the lectures. A known problem with many software engineering courses taught in the past is that students become involved with the project they are implementing, and ignore the material in lecture. This has been partially addressed by including a large number of (hopefully) interesting topics not usually taught in software engineering courses.

- The software engineering course currently taught was studied as a basis [58].

11.3.7. Software Engineering Lab [414]

Prerequisites: vary with the individual arrangement
SOFTWARE ENGINEERING [413]

Description: This course is intended to provide a vehicle for real-world software engineering experience. Students will work on existing software that is or will soon be in service. In a work environment, a student will experience first-hand the pragmatic arguments for proper design, documentation, and other software practices that often seem to have hollow rationalizations when applied to code that a student writes for an assignment and then never uses again. Projects and supervision will be individually arranged.

Rationale: Software engineering issues arise in software that involves many months, many programmers, many versions, and many modules. These issues are extremely hard to raise in a one-semester course; they are easier to appreciate by working with real-world projects. This course is intended to provide an opportunity for training similar to a clinical practice course in a medical school. This will require closer cooperation between the industrial work site and the university than an ordinary work-study program would need. Evaluation of students will be shared between university faculty and the individual(s) managing them in the industrial organization.

Objectives: At the end of this course, a student will be able to:

  ► Apply software engineering principles to large, long-term projects

  ► Work effectively in a programming team

Ideas: This course will be the primary carrier of the following:

  ► Complexity of real-world systems

  ► Tools for dealing with that complexity

Implementation Considerations and Concerns:

  ► Getting good projects and good supervision. The people who serve as faculty for this course must be selected carefully.

  ► We must be careful not to have this become a "mindless programming for credit" course; the students must work on challenging projects that will force them to work with practicing software engineers.

11.3.8. Transducers of Programs [420]

Prerequisites: PROGRAM ORGANIZATIONS [313]
                LANGUAGES, INTERFACES, AND THEIR PROCESSORS [320]

Description: This course studies ways to gain leverage on the software development process by using programs to create or modify other programs, by reusing previously-created software, and by using automated tools to manage the software development process. Examples are drawn from the tools locally available. Students use these tools in projects that lead to useful software components. Special emphasis is placed on the use of integrated systems of compatible tools.

Rationale: As programming is usually taught, students often form the impression that programs are always created from scratch, by hand. The major theme of this course is that programs are frequently created by and from other programs, and that this leverage is important in increasing productivity and in transmitting good techniques in the form of working software, not just by word of mouth. More specifically, a system of any size can often be factored into segments, some of which have a structure so standard that they can be build from a specification by a specialized tool.

For example, parser generators are used as tools in the prerequisite course LANGUAGES, INTERFACES, AND THEIR PROCESSORS [320] with only a cursory introduction to the techniques encapsulated in the tool. In this course, such tools are the objects of study and, for example, the practical parsing theory needed to understand, modify, or even construct a parser or parser-generator is included. In similar fashion, this course covers libraries (both design and administration), program development environments, smart editors, and other mechanisms for using programs to construct or maintain programs. More compiler components are studied, and many of the examples are drawn from the class of tools that can be easily integrated in a system surrounding a parse-tree representation of programs.

Objectives: At the end of this course, a student will be able to:

▶ Use automated tools effectively in software development.

▶ Describe the organization of a compiler and make minor modifications to one.

▶ Add compatible tools to a unified program development system, taking advantage of existing components and using interface representations correctly.

Ideas: This course will be the primary carrier of the following:

▶ Internal representations for compilation and the possibility of using them as an interface medium

- ► Tools for program development, especially tool-building tools
- ► Relation between complexity of language and complexity of implementation; interaction of language design and system issues
- ► Compiler organization as example of medium-large system
- ► Parsing and code generation

It will reinforce or share responsibility for:

- ► Various classes of languages and their power (and the cost of processing them)
- ► Relation between syntax and semantics
- ► Duality between programs and data
- ► Practical application of formal theories

Topic Outline:

1. Reusable software

- ► Libraries and integrated packages—strengths and weaknesses
- ► Certified software (e.g., the math software)
- ► Specifications
- ► Evolution: building programs by modifying similar programs
- ► Program transformation

2. Tools for operating on programs

- ► Classes of tools, such as
  - > Tools that help you program (editors, cross-referencers, etc)
  - > Tools that help you organize programs into systems (filters, system modellers, etc)
  - > Tools that build programs (parser generators, etc)

- ► Programmable editors and filters
- ► Generic definitions
- ► Program transformations and history editors
- ► Test data generators
- ► Verification condition generation systems

3. Techniques and concepts for implementation of tools

- ► Parsing techniques
- ► Families of representations shared by integrated tools

4. Use of integrated tools

- ► Examples: whatever's available locally from tools in the spirit of Gandalf, programmer's workbench, etc. Most likely, this will be a set of tools that operate on the parse-tree representation of a program
- ► Tools: editors, program development database, documentation generators, version control/system modelling tools

5. Construction of integrated tools

▶ What goes on inside a front-end generator?

> Example connects to previous course LANGUAGES, INTERFACES, AND THEIR PROCESSORS [320]

> Practical parsing theory—why the limitations on the grammars arise

> How that theory is used in (and affects) the implementation

▶ Bootstrapping

6. Projects:

▶ Students should have a project in which they must factor a system into segments that can be generated by tools.

▶ Students should write a simple tool to produce code from specifications for simple factored segments.

▶ These two parts of the project should be coupled to prior study of one or more examples in considerable depth.

References:

▶ A.V. Aho and J.D. Ullman, *Principles of Compiler Design* [5]. (The "Dragon Book")

▶ D. Gries, *Compiler Construction for Digital Computers* [43].

▶ *Proceedings of the Workshop on Reusability in Programming* [56].

▶ B.W. Kernighan and P.J. Plauger, *Software Tools in Pascal* [59].

Resource Requirements:

▶ Software development tools to form a laboratory that is both rich enough to illustrate the principles and simple enough for undergraduate course projects.

▶ A demonstration compiler for students to modify.

▶ Examples of useful subroutine libraries.

Implementation Considerations and Concerns:

▶ This course is at present a bit speculative. We believe that enough material already exists to teach it now, but this part of the discipline is developing rapidly. It is important to be sure that the course remains flexible for a few years so that the best of current understanding can be included.

▶ In the short run, parser generators provide the best example of automatable tools with solid theoretical underpinning. For the time being, perhaps as much as 20% of the course could be devoted to parsing techniques, but this share should be expected to decrease as other tools emerge.

11.3.9. Advanced Programming Languages and Compilers [421]

Prerequisites: FORMAL LANGUAGES, AUTOMATA, AND COMPLEXITY [350]
INTRODUCTION TO ARTIFICIAL INTELLIGENCE [360]
TRANSDUCERS OF PROGRAMS [420]

Description: This course is intended for students seriously interested in the construction of compilers for general-purpose programming languages. The student studies an optimizing compiler as an example of a well-organized system program, studies algorithms and data structures appropriate to the optimization process, examines code generators, optimizers, and their interactions. The student also studies comparative programming languages with emphasis on the interaction between language design and implementation considerations. Compiler-generator technology is used to build a compiler, thereby demonstrating the use of system-building tools.

Rationale: This is the third course derived from the traditional compiler course (the rational for the sequence is given in the description of LANGUAGES, INTERFACES, AND THEIR PROCESSORS [320]). Techniques that are broadly useful for interfaces to interactive programs have been moved into LANGUAGES, INTERFACES, AND THEIR PROCESSORS [320]. Techniques for which good automated tools exist have been at least introduced in TRANSDUCERS OF PROGRAMS [420]. This course addresses the techniques that are specialized to optimizing compilers. In addition to the traditional content, it will cover the use of automated tools for compiler construction and advanced language design topics.

Objectives: At the end of this course, a student will be able to:

► Participate competently in the construction of production-quality compilers using modern compiler-construction techniques and tools

► Identify language features and combinations of features that constrain or simplify implementation

Ideas: This course will be the primary carrier of the following:

► Understanding implementation techniques for programming languages

► Using new data structures introduced in the course

► Applying new tools introduced in the course

It will reinforce or share responsibility for:

► Understanding the components of a medium-sized system and how they interact

► Programming language design issues

► Applying theoretical techniques in practice

Topic Outline:

1. Compiler as an example of a complex medium-sized system
2. Intermediate representations for processing programs
3. Compiler-compiler technology
4. Implementation issues for programming languages

   ▶ Lexical analysis, parsing, and semantic analysis (revisited)
   ▶ Code generation
   ▶ Global program analysis and optimization
   ▶ Optimization
   ▶ Interpretation
   ▶ Storage allocation, garbage collection
   ▶ Input/output

5. Techniques applied

   ▶ AI search techniques
   ▶ Graph theory
   ▶ Data flow
   ▶ Others reflecting current research

6. Advanced topics in programming language organization and design

   ▶ Interaction among design decisions (parameter binding rules, rules for assignment, etc.)
   ▶ Interaction between language design decisions and implementations
   ▶ Kinds of programming languages (survey)
     > General-purpose programming languages
     > Applicative vs. imperative
     > Assemblers, macros
     > Very high-level languages
     > Systems implementation languages
     > Special-purpose languages
     > Production systems
     > Object-oriented languages
     > Query languages
     > Graphical interaction
     > Special-purpose and application-based systems

References:

▶ A.V. Aho and J.D. Ullman, *Principles of Compiler Design* [5]. (The "Dragon Book")
▶ Alan Feuer and Narain Gehani (editors), *Comparing and Assessing Programming Languages* [35].
▶ D. Gries, *Compiler Construction for Digital Computers* [43].

▸ R.L. Wexelblat, *History of Programming Languages* [121].

▸ W. Wulf et al. *The Design of an Optimizing Compiler* [126]

Resource Requirements (software):

▸ Automatic generators for compiler components such as lexical analyzers and parsers.

▸ Instances of other components of a compiler (symbol table module, various optimization modules)

▸ The objective is a software lab similar to a physics lab: the student "checks out" selected apparatus for an experiment, then assembles it and measures the result.

Implementation Considerations and Concerns:

▸ The balance between language design and compiler implementation must be carefully preserved.

11.3.10. Advanced Algorithms [430]

Prerequisites: ALGORITHMS AND PROGRAMS [330]
COMBINATORIAL ANALYSIS [MATH 301 / CS 251]

Description: A second course in the design and analysis of algorithms.

Rationale: This course is intended to familiarize the student with the unifying principles and underlying concepts of algorithm design and analysis. It extends and refines the algorithmic concepts introduced in ALGORITHMS AND PROGRAMS [330]. Here a more abstract view is taken, with emphasis on the fundamental ideas of problem diagnosis, design of algorithms, and analysis. The course assumes familiarity with material on combinatorial analysis.

Objectives: At the end of this course, a student will be able to:

- ▶ Design efficient algorithms
- ▶ Analyze the performance of algorithms

Ideas: This course will be the primary carrier of the following:

- ▶ Lower bounds
- ▶ Optimization

It will reinforce or share responsibility for:

- ▶ Analysis of algorithms
- ▶ Complexity theory

Topic Outline:

1. **Data structures**
   - ▶ Lower bound arguments
   - ▶ Recurrences
   - ▶ Union-find

2. **Graph algorithms**
   - ▶ Topological sort
   - ▶ Biconnectivity
   - ▶ Matching
   - ▶ Maximum flow

3. **Algebraic algorithms**
   - ▶ Strassen's algorithm
   - ▶ Transitive closure
   - ▶ Chinese remainder algorithm
   - ▶ Four Russians' algorithm
   - ▶ Fast Fourier transform
   - ▶ Power series multiplication/division

▸ Lower bound arguments

4. Linear programming

5. Complexity theory

6. Approximation algorithms

References:

▸ A.V. Aho, J.D. Hopcroft, and J.E. Ullman, *The Design and Analysis of Computer Algorithms* [4].

▸ J.A. Bondy and U.S.R. Murty, *Graph Theory with Applications* [14].

▸ F. Harary, *Graph Theory* [47].

▸ D.E. Knuth, *The Art of Computer Programming* [60, 64, 61].

▸ E.L. Lawler, *Combinatorial Optimization* [67].

▸ C.H. Papadimitriou and K. Steiglitz, *Combinatorial Optimization* [87].

Implementation Considerations and Concerns:

▸ In addition to the ALGORITHMS AND PROGRAMS [330] prerequisite, this course also requires students to possess mathematical maturity. This requirement should be aided by the prerequisite COMBINATORIAL ANALYSIS [MATH 301 / CS 251].

▸ There is considerable overlap between this course the material of APPLIED GRAPH THEORY [MATH 484].

11.3.11. Computer Architecture [440]

Prerequisites: TIME AND RESOURCES [310]
                    or INTRODUCTION TO DIGITAL SYSTEMS [EE 133]

Description: This course teaches the important concepts in computer system
   hardware design. System architecture is the focus of this course, so the
   technological details of the components from which such systems are
   constructed are avoided except where they are crucial to design goals like
   capacity and performance. The topics that are taught include design
   models including the register transfer level (RTL) model, instruction set
   processor (ISP) model, and processor-memory-switch (PMS) model.
   Analytic tools taught include notions of quantity of data based on
   information theory, queueing theory concepts, and performance
   evaluation techniques.

Rationale: A computer scientist ought to understand the design decisions
   that are embodied in the computers that he uses for the same reasons that
   an automobile driver ought to understand his vehicle: a user who
   understands his tool can make better use of its capabilities. As a course
   that focuses exclusively on hardware, this course will teach the computer
   scientist things about his machines that a simple understanding of
   computability and complexity does not provide. As a first exposure to
   machine architecture, this course will prepare the machine architect for
   more complex concepts in computer engineering.

Objectives: At the end of this course, a student will be able to:

► Understand and apply architectural techniques in design and
   analysis of systems

Ideas: This course will be the primary carrier of the following:

► Machine Architecture design techniques: RTL, ISP, PMS

► System resources: disks, tapes, drums, memory, I/O devices

► Data communication—coding, quantity of information

► Performance evaluation

It will reinforce or share responsibility for:

► Finite-state machines

► Addressing, data representation, and storage

► Analysis, synthesis, and evaluation

Topic Outline:

1. Assembly language

   ► Instruction set (68000 as sample)

   ► Instruction formats

   ► Addressing schemes

▶ An assembler programming project

2. **Arithmetic logic unit (ALU) design**

   ▶ Addition and subtraction

   ▶ Multiplication and division

   ▶ Other ALU functions (masks, flags, etc.)

   ▶ Floating point representations (add, subtract, multiply, divide, fast ALUs, multiplier units)

3. **Central processor design**

   ▶ Register schemes (stack, one address, two address, three address)

   ▶ Instruction formats

   ▶ Pipelining

   ▶ Lookahead and parallelism

4. **Memory**

   ▶ Primary memory design

   ▶ Interleaved memory

   ▶ Secondary memory

   ▶ Associative memory

5. **Memory management**

   ▶ Memory hierarchies

   ▶ Paging systems

   ▶ Segmented systems

   ▶ Replacement algorithms

   ▶ Cache memories

6. **The control unit**

   ▶ Microprogramming

   ▶ Hardwired control

7. **Input/output (I/O)**

   ▶ Memory mapped vs. programmed I/O

   ▶ Direct memory access (DMA)

   ▶ Channel I/O

   ▶ I/O modelling

8. **Some design examples**

   ▶ PDP-11

   ▶ IBM 370

   ▶ HP 3000

9. **Data communication and information theory**

   ▶ Quantity of information, entropy

   ▶ Signals and noise

- ▶ Shannon's theorem
- ▶ Error correcting codes

10. Performance evaluation

- ▶ Queuing models
- ▶ Markov chains
- ▶ Simulation, measurement

References:

- ▶ C.G. Bell, J.C. Mudge, and J.E. McNamara, *Computer Engineering* [8].
- ▶ D.P. Siewiorek, C.G. Bell, and A. Newell, *Computer Structures: Principles and Examples* [106].

Implementation Considerations and Concerns:

- ▶ This course is also listed as INTRODUCTION TO COMPUTER ARCHITECTURE [EE 247] in the Electrical Engineering Department.

11.3.12. VLSI Systems [441]

Prerequisites: COMPUTER ARCHITECTURE [440]
ALGORITHMS AND PROGRAMS [330]

Description: This course introduces the technology of VLSI and its use in system design. A broad survey of current technologies and simple design methodologies is given. The emphasis throughout is on practical issues, and the student will learn how to design projects and implement them on a chip. After introducing the basics of VLSI, the course goes on to consider aspects of system design using VLSI.

Rationale: VLSI technology is assuming increasing importance as an aid to high performance, low cost system design. Computer scientists should be familiar with the advantages, possibilities and limitations of such an important technology.

Objectives: At the end of this course, a student will be able to design and implement simple projects in VLSI, and should be well prepared for more advanced work in this area.

Ideas: This course will be the primary carrier of the following:

- ▶ VLSI technology, NMOS, CMOS
- ▶ Fabrication and design of chips

It will reinforce or share responsibility for:

- ▶ Logic design
- ▶ Design techniques for computer hardware
- ▶ Clocked and self-timed systems
- ▶ Hardware synchronization circuits
- ▶ Finite-state machines

Topic Outline:

1. **IC technology and design methods**

   ▶ A brief summary of integrated circuit technology and design methods.

2. **MOS transistors**

   ▶ Common NMOS and CMOS device structures and their principles of operation.

3. **Gates**

   ▶ Ratioed NMOS and ratioless CMOS logic gates, including inverters, NAND, NOR and XOR
   ▶ CMOS transmission gates
   ▶ Precharging and Domino CMOS logic
   ▶ Static and transient behavior of gates
   ▶ Switch-level and logical abstractions

4. **Fabrication and design rules**

   ► A typical MOS fabrication process, with simple NMOS and CMOS design rules.

   ► Examples of gate layouts.

   ► CAD tools for layout.

5. **CIF: a geometric language**

   ► The standard geometrical interchange format is described to show how geometry is specified. Layout analysis tools such as circuit extractors and wirelist comparators are introduced and used.

6. **Clocked logic and shift registers**

7. **Combinational logic between latches**

   ► Dynamic latches and their use in logic design.

8. **Type D static latches (flip-flops)**

   ► The concepts of static logic and positive feedback are introduced.

9. **Programmable logic arrays and ROMs**

   ► Examples of PLAs

   ► CAD tools for transforming logic equations to PLAs

   ► ROMs as fully-populated PLAs, and PLAs as sparse ROMs.

   ► Logic minimization

10. **Finite state machines**

   ► Finite state machines are described, along with their implementation using PLAs. CAD tools for designing finite state machines are mentioned.

11. **Synchronous system timing**

   ► Strategies for clocked-system design, along with clock distribution.

12. **Clocks and clock generators**

   ► Circuits for clock generation, oscillators, bootstrapped drivers, etc.

13. **Self-timing**

   ► Basic ideas of self-timed systems, with a few simple example circuits.

14. **Testability and testing**

   ► Circuit faults, and strategies for detecting them.

   ► Logic to aid testability, such as LSSD.

   ► Self-testing

   ► Fault simulators and test pattern generation

15. **RAMs**

   ► Circuit techniques for static and dynamic RAM design.

   ► A simple static RAM for use in student designs.

16. **Special purpose VLSI architectures**

   ► Systolic arrays

   ► Simple examples of systolic algorithms

References:

- ► C. Mead and L. Conway, *Introduction to VLSI Systems* [77].
- ► J. D. Ullman, *Computational Aspects of VLSI* [117].

Resource Requirements:

- ► Locally accessible on-line tools for design and testing
- ► Access to fabrication facilities

Implementation Considerations and Concerns:

- ► The best way to learn to do VLSI design is to do VLSI design. Therefore, the life blood of the course should be design projects. Two would be typical: one that is fairly simple such as a flip-flop, shift register or counter, and one that is more advanced. Access to facilities for testing and fabrication of chips will be vital here. There is a potential for a serious scheduling problem here, since chip designs must be tested before fabrication and there may be considerable turn-around delays during fabrication.
- ► It is a great help in teaching this course to have ready access to computer-aided design tools of various kinds. The outline as presented above introduces a wide range of CAD tools in sequence.
- ► The course outline as given above owes very much to the first reference book by Mead and Conway. The Ullman book has a rather different emphasis and should be regarded as providing a supplement to the course material.
- ► This course may need to be reassessed and redesigned as VLSI design techniques and technologies develop. If the course is going to concentrate solely on either NMOS or on CMOS, then only the appropriate topics need be selected from the outline.
- ► It might be an advantage to bring the course into an earlier position in the curriculum plan, or to try to integrate its contents better with the other system design courses. This would allow a later, more advanced course to be offered which assumed more knowledge of electrical engineering material and computer science basics.

11.3.13. Theory of Programming Languages [450]

Prerequisites: LANGUAGES, INTERFACES, AND THEIR PROCESSORS [320]
              FORMAL LANGUAGES, AUTOMATA, AND COMPLEXITY [350]
              LOGIC FOR COMPUTER SCIENCE [351]

Description: This course brings together fundamental material on the theory
    of programming languages. Techniques for assigning mathematical
    meanings to programs and for reasoning precisely about program
    functionality and behavior are described. Some indication is given of the
    influence of formal methods on programming methodology and
    programming language design.

Rationale: Programs are rarely verified formally in practice, but there is
    much to be learned—both about programming techniques and about
    programming language design—from a study of precise methods for
    reasoning about programs. Indeed, we cannot reason precisely about
    programs unless we have a sound mathematical basis for such reasoning;
    this course is intended to provide that foundation.

Objectives: The student should gain from this course an understanding of the
    variety of approaches and techniques to reasoning precisely about
    programs. In particular, students should appreciate the potential for
    automation of these techniques, the ways in which they might be applied
    in practice, and their theoretical limitations.

Ideas: This course will be the primary carrier of the following:

- ▸ Formal reasoning about programs.
- ▸ Semantics of programming languages.
- ▸ Assertions about programs.

It will reinforce or share responsibility for:

- ▸ Programming methodology.
- ▸ Specifications of programs.
- ▸ Programming language design.

Topic Outline:

1. **Introduction to semantics of programming languages**

  - ▸ Syntax, semantics, and pragmatics: the distinctions
  - ▸ Abstract syntax and formal semantics
  - ▸ Assigning meanings to programs
  - ▸ Operational semantics
    - > Compilers and interpreters
    - > Labelled transition systems
    - > Operational semantics for simple sequential language with loops

- ▶ Denotational semantics
  - > Basic idea: semantics given by structural induction
  - > Foundations: domains, continuous functions, and fixed points
  - > Semantics of a simple language
  - > Congruence between operational and denotational semantics

- ▶ Axiomatic semantics
  - > Hoare-style axioms
  - > Weakest preconditions and predicate transformers
  - > Axiomatic semantics for simple language
  - > Consistency with respect to denotational or operational semantics
  - > Elementary ideas of soundness and relative completeness

2. **The variety of programming languages**
   - ▶ The distinction between imperative and applicative programs
   - ▶ The distinction between environment and store
   - ▶ Lazy evaluation and infinite structures
   - ▶ Object-oriented programming languages
   - ▶ Very-high-level programming languages

3. **Semantic treatment of more complicated programming constructs:**
   - ▶ Procedures:
     - > Parameterless
     - > Recursion
     - > Methods of parameter passing

   - ▶ Jumps (goto statement, breaks, etc.)
   - ▶ Nondeterminism (e.g., Dijkstra's guarded commands)
   - ▶ Parallelism:
     - > Treatment as nondeterministic interleaving of actions
     - > Concurrent processes (eg. CSP, CCS, ADA)
     - > Coroutines

   - ▶ Continuation semantics
   - ▶ Relational semantics
   - ▶ Elementary ideas of powerdomain semantics

4. **Reasoning about programs**
   - ▶ Inductive proof techniques
     - > Structural induction
     - > Well-founded induction
     - > Computational induction

- ▸ Partial correctness
    - \> Flowcharts and inductive assertions
    - \> Hoare-style assertions
    - \> Weakest preconditions
- ▸ Total correctness of sequential programs
    - \> Proving termination: examples of well-founded sets
    - \> The sometime method
    - \> Weakest liberal preconditions
- ▸ Fixed-point properties of recursive programs
- ▸ Temporal logic
    - \> Continuously-operating programs
- ▸ Dynamic logic

5. **Manipulating programs**

- ▸ Equivalence of programs
- ▸ Program transformations and their correctness

References:

- ▸ E.W. Dijkstra, *A Discipline of Programming* [31].
- ▸ M.J.C. Gordon, *The Denotational Description of Programming Languages.* [41].
- ▸ Z. Manna, *The Mathematical Theory of Computation* [75].
- ▸ J.E. Stoy, *Denotational Semantics: The Scott-Strachey Approach to Programming Language Theory* [110].
- ▸ R.D. Tennent, *Principles of Programming Languages* [113].

Implementation Considerations and Concerns:

- ▸ We have included a long list of important topics, from which it is possible to draw a variety of particular courses tailored to special needs or interests. At this advanced level, it is appropriate to allow some freedom in the selection of appropriate course material, especially since the area we are covering here is not yet static.
- ▸ This type of course would benefit greatly from a computer-aided facility for semantic test-bedding of formal definitions, such as symbolic execution. Although not necessary for the implementation of the course, such tools would help.

11.3.14. Complexity Theory [451]

Prerequisites: ALGORITHMS AND PROGRAMS [330]
             FORMAL LANGUAGES, AUTOMATA, AND COMPLEXITY [350]
             COMBINATORIAL ANALYSIS [MATH 301 / CS 251]

Description: This course extends in much more detail the material first
introduced in FORMAL LANGUAGES, AUTOMATA, AND COMPLEXITY
[350]. After a quick review of the basic ideas of complexity theory, the
course introduces some of the advanced results and open questions of
abstract complexity theory, and the techniques used in proving these
results. Emphasis is made on relating these results and open questions to
their theoretical and practical implications for computer science; the
study of computability leads to theoretical limitations on what a computer
can in principle (given enough time and space) do, while the study of
complexity yields limitations on what is feasibly computable: if we are
restricted to using only a limited amount of time or space, the class of
problems solvable by computer is restricted. There is some similarity of
course content with THEORY OF ALGORITHMS [MATH 451].

Rationale: The theory of complexity is an interesting area in which many
important problems remain to be solved. This course serves the purpose
of engaging the student's interest and equipping him with the
background material and ideas necessary for tackling research in this area.

Objectives: At the end of this course, a student will have a feeling for the
theoretical limitations of computers, and how restrictions on working
space and running time affect the capability of computers to solve
problems. He will have seen enough of the methods and results of this
subject to enable him to tackle research in this growing area.

Ideas: This course will be the primary carrier of the following:

- ▶ Time and space hierarchies
- ▶ Notions of reducibility
- ▶ Complete sets for problem classes
- ▶ Implications of the $P = NP$ problem

It will reinforce or share responsibility for:

- ▶ Time and space tradeoffs
- ▶ Diagonal arguments
- ▶ Algorithms

Topic Outline:

1. **Review of elementary complexity theory:**
   - ▶ Distinction between computability and complexity
   - ▶ Space complexity and time complexity
   - ▶ Complexity relative to deterministic and nondeterministic computation

2. The time and space hierarchies: P, NP, co-NP, PSPACE, etc.

3. Time vs. space trade-offs

4. Location of known problems in the hierarchy: graph isomorphism, recognition problems, etc.

5. Notions of reducibility:

   ▶ Turing reducibility

   ▶ Polynomial reducibility

   ▶ Logspace reducibility

   ▶ Use of reductions to show complexity properties

6. Complete sets for NP: 3CNF, Clique, Hamiltonian circuits

7. Complete sets for PSPACE: QBF

8. Conditions that would imply P = NP

9. Implications for computer science of the P = NP question: what is the class of "feasibly computable" problems?

10. Computability and complexity relative to an oracle

References:

▶ M.R. Garey and D.S. Johnson, *Computers and Intractability: A Guide to the Theory of NP-Completeness* [38].

▶ J.E. Hopcroft and J.D. Ullman, *Introduction to Automata Theory, Languages and Computation* [53].

▶ H. Rogers, *Theory of Recursive Functions and Effective Computability* [98].

Implementation Considerations and Concerns:

▶ The material covered in this course overlaps with the content of THEORY OF ALGORITHMS [MATH 451].

11.3.15. Artificial Intelligence—Cognitive Processes [460]

Prerequisites: INTRODUCTION TO ARTIFICIAL INTELLIGENCE [360]
Another course in Cognitive Psychology is strongly
recommended

Description: Covers more advanced aspects of the cognitive side of AI, including natural language processing, use of knowledge sources, and learning and discovery. The use of computer programs as psychological models will also be discussed. Students will implement a large AI system as a semester project. Its primary objective is to immerse the student in the design and construction of a substantial AI system on a topic of his or her choice.

Rationale: This course covers the symbolic side of AI, and allows for interaction between computer science students and psychology students. The semester project is here rather than in the prerequisite course, because the prerequisite, INTRODUCTION TO ARTIFICIAL INTELLIGENCE [360], has a lot of ground to cover and little time in which to do it, and because most of the prerequisite material should be digested before the student spends too much time on a project.

Objectives: At the end of this course, a student will be able to:

- Use computer programs to model psychological phenomena
- Write large AI systems, such as expert systems, natural language interpreters, simulation systems, and knowledge-rich problem solvers.

Ideas: This course will be the primary carrier of the following:

- Cognitive simulation
- Machine Learning
- Natural language processing
- Complex problem solving techniques requiring the integration of multiple knowledge sources.

It will reinforce or share responsibility for:

- Knowledge representation (shared with BIG DATA [410] and INTRODUCTION TO ARTIFICIAL INTELLIGENCE [360])

Topic Outline:
1. **Techniques**
    - Exploiting constraints
    - Heuristic programming
    - Production systems
    - Extended weak methods
    - Knowledge intensive methods

   ▶ Problem solving architectures (e.g. blackboard model, inference engines, horn-clause resolution)

2. **Knowledge representation**

   ▶ Declarative knowledge

   ▶ Inference and inheritance

   ▶ Procedural knowledge

   ▶ Episodic knowledge and scripts

   ▶ Semantic nets

3. **Natural language**

   ▶ ATN parsing

   ▶ Case-frame parsing

   ▶ Text Generation

4. **Expert systems**

   ▶ Design

   ▶ Engineering analysis

   ▶ Diagnosis systems

5. **Cognitive processes**

   ▶ Concept acquisition

   ▶ Discovery

   ▶ Machine learning

   ▶ Planning

   ▶ Analogical reasoning

References:

   ▶ E. Charniak, C.K. Riesbeck, and D.V. McDermott, *Artificial Intelligence Programming* [19]

   ▶ N.J. Nilsson, *Principles of Artificial Intelligence* [84]

   ▶ E. Rich, *Artificial Intelligence* [97]

   ▶ R.C. Schank and C.K. Riesbeck, *Inside Computer Understanding* [100].

Resource Requirements:

   ▶ Online versions of McEli, McSam, etc.

   ▶ Lisp programming environment with lots of high quality Lisp cycles (e.g. Lisp machines, MacLisp, Franz Lisp, Interlisp, or Common Lisp)

   ▶ Lab assistants to supervise individual projects

Implementation Considerations and Concerns:

   ▶ INTRODUCTION TO ARTIFICIAL INTELLIGENCE [360] is a hard

prerequisite. All students must be proficient Lisp programmers for this course to work.

11.3.16. Artificial Intelligence—Robotics [461]

Prerequisites: INTRODUCTION TO ROBOTICS [361]
   Other prerequisites vary with the instructor and project

Description: This course is intended to provide actual experience in development of robotic systems. Students, individually or in a group, will work on a small task in vision, speech, robot programming, manipulation, locomotion, and other robotics topics.

Rationale: Learning robotics requires hands-on experience. Students have to develop a feeling for dealing with actual physical-world phenomena — real-time processing, noise, stability, etc., which is hard to acquire from a classroom study.   The Carnegie-Mellon Computer Science/Robotics Institute community has a large body of expertise in this area. We can ask faculty to participate in this course by providing appropriate tasks and supervising students. Students will develop the best understanding of the subjects by actually working with researchers.

Objectives: At the end of this course, a student will be able to:

- Apply basic knowledge and techniques in robotics, Artificial Intelligence, and programming to a specific robotics task.
- Appreciate the difficulty and the importance of dealing with the physical world.

Ideas: This course will be the primary carrier of the following:

- Skill and techniques in developing perception (vision/speech) and other robotic systems.

Topic Outline:
Topics will be selected from available robotics projects.

Resource Requirements:

- This course needs a dedicated laboratory and computing facilities with appropriate devices, including an image display device and an arm for experiment. University computing facilities may therefore be inadequate. For example, all the low level-system capabilities for vision, such as image file format and pixel access must be prepared.
- The minimum lab/system configuration for the course will be:
  > Vax 11/780
  > A printer for images and/or good high-resolution raster display
  > A manipulator
  > (possibly) Workbench, basic electronics parts/tools, measurement equipment

> (possibly) A TV camera and image digitizer

Without such resources this course should not be offered, unless the instructor is able to accommodate the course work in his own research project environment.

▶ Implementation Considerations and Concerns:

> This course could be very expensive in terms of facilities and faculty time. Therefore, it must be carefully planned by the individual instructor, and high-quality must be maintained. Otherwise, the course should not be offered.

> The instructor should prepare the tasks very carefully. The goal, prerequisites, and grading criteria must be clearly defined.

> Only a small number of students that are clearly qualified should be admitted.

> Topics and instructors can be solicited from the Computer Science/Robotics Institute community.

11.3.17. Interactive Graphics Techniques [470]

Prerequisites: LANGUAGES, INTERFACES, AND THEIR PROCESSORS [320]
ALGORITHMS AND PROGRAMS [330]

Description: A course in the creation and use of graphical information and
user-interfaces.

Rationale: Although relatively young, the field of graphics has consolidated
enough to warrant a semester course centering on the use of graphical,
rather than textual, interaction with computers. As graphical display
devices become more widespread, it becomes increasingly vital to know
how to use them effectively. A fair amount of background is required;
students will have to apply previously learned material from areas
including algorithms and language models of interaction.

Objectives: At the end of this course, a student will be able to:

- ▶ Create interactive interfaces for computer applications.
- ▶ Understand the basic implementation and use of graphic support packages.
- ▶ Evaluate ergonomic aspects of user interfaces.

Ideas: This course will be the primary carrier of the following:

- ▶ The concept of graphical vs. textual interaction.
- ▶ Graphical interface creation principles.
- ▶ A knowledge basis to judge the merits of existing graphical tools.

Topic Outline:

1. History of computer graphics
2. Current applications
3. Graphics hardware
    - ▶ Vector graphics vs. raster graphics
    - ▶ RasterOp
    - ▶ Input devices (logical and real)
    - ▶ Possible future developments
4. Fundamental graphics operations
    - ▶ Coordinate system specification and mappings
    - ▶ Scan-conversion of lines and splines
    - ▶ Clipping
    - ▶ Transformation and homogeneous coordinates
5. Use of graphics packages
    - ▶ Intermediate description formats for graphical information
    - ▶ Device independence
    - ▶ CORE and GKS

6. **Implementation of graphics packages**

7. **Interaction techniques**

  ▶ Menu driven systems

  ▶ Rubber banding, gravity, constraints, icons, dragging

  ▶ Modeless vs. moded interaction

  ▶ FSA model, table-driven applications

  ▶ Prompting, confirmation, error-checking, undo, redo, consistency

  ▶ Prefix, postfix, infix operations

  ▶ Window-based systems

8. **User-computer dialogue**

  ▶ Language considerations

  ▶ Human factors

9. **Three (and greater) dimensional viewing**

  ▶ Specification

  ▶ Implementation

  ▶ Solid-modelling systems

10. **Graphical algorithms**

  ▶ Polygonal scan-conversion

  ▶ Hidden line/surface removal, shading, lighting models

  ▶ "Painting" algorithms, including seedfill and airbrush

11. **Color models and the use of color**

12. **Hard-copy graphics output**

  ▶ phototypesetters

  ▶ bitmapped printers

  ▶ isometric plots

  ▶ half-toning

References:

  ▶ J.D. Foley and A. van Dam, *Fundamentals of Interactive Computer Graphics* [37].

  ▶ W.M. Newman and R.F. Sproull, *Principles of Interactive Computer Graphics* [82].

Resource Requirements:

  ▶ Various sorts of graphical devices for both display and input

  ▶ Implementations of existing graphics packages

  ▶ Example interfaces

  ▶ Computational support for some fairly compute-intensive operations

Implementation Considerations and Concerns:

▸ There has been a great deal of discussion about whether there should be two courses involving graphics. One would be intended primarily for "users" of graphics packages and utilities, the other for "creators" of these. The second course would presumably have the first as a prerequisite. At this time, attempts to sketch out two separate courses gave the impression that the existing body of material was too small to form two courses, but that in several years this would probably change. Towards that end, topics 1, 2, 3, 5, 7, 8, 11, and 12 of the current outline are expected to become part of the first course when the split occurs.

12. Related Courses

This chapter contains descriptions of related courses in mathematics, statistics, electrical engineering, cognitive psychology, management, and public policy. They are included here because of their close ties to courses described in the previous chapter. In addition, they may be of interest for constructing concentrations in fields allied to computer science.

Some of the courses in this chapter are not currently offered, but are rather sketches of courses that sound interesting to us. These should be interpreted as proposals for discussion.

The numbers for these courses are the numbers used at Carnegie-Mellon. They are unlikely to correspond to the numbering schemes of other schools; they are used here merely to provide unique identification.

12.1. Mathematics Courses

12.1.1. Introduction to Discrete Mathematics [Math 127 / CS 150]

An outline for this course is given in Section 11.1.3.

12.1.2. Calculus I [Math 121]

Description: Functions, limits, derivatives of algebraic, trigonometric, exponential and logarithmic functions, curve sketching, related rate and maximum-minimum problems, definite and indefinite integrals with applications. [CMU course 21-121]

12.1.3. Calculus II [Math 122]

Description: Techniques of integration, improper integrals, Taylor's series, functions of several variables, partial derivatives, directional derivatives, chain-rule, the gradient, multiple integrals, line integrals. Prerequisite: CALCULUS I [MATH 121]. [CMU course 21-122]

12.1.4. Methods of Applied Math I [Math 259]

Description: Ordinary Differential Equations: first-order, second order linear, input-output analysis, Fourier series, power series methods, Laplace transform methods. Matrix algebra, eigenvalues, systems of differential equations. Prerequisite: CALCULUS II [MATH 122] [CMU course 21-259]

12.1.5. Elements of Analysis [Math 261]

Description: Functions of several variables, chain-rule, inverse function theorem, coordinates, multiple integrals. Vector analysis: line and surface integrals, divergence and Stokes' theorems. Convergence of series and sequences, Taylor's series, Fourier series. Prerequisite: METHODS OF APPLIED MATH I [MATH 259]. [CMU course 21-261]

12.1.6. Operations Research I [Math 292]

Description: The distribution-transportation problem: row and column number solution method and sensitivity analysis; flows in networks and incidence matrices; the standard linear program; the simplex method, post-optimality and the economic lot size problem; dynamic programming and the knapsack problem; introduction to queueing. Prerequisite: CALCULUS II [MATH 122]. [CMU course 21-292]

12.1.7. Operations Research II [Math 293]

Description: Extension of linear programming, integer programming, game theory; probabilistic programming; case studies from economics, engineering and management science. Prerequisite: OPERATIONS RESEARCH I [MATH 292] [CMU course 21-293]

12.1.8. Combinatorial Analysis [Math 301 / CS 251]

Description: An introduction to combinatorial mathematics with an emphasis on applications in computer science. Topics covered in depth include permutations and combinations, generating functions, recurrence relations, the principle of inclusion and exclusion, and the Fibonacci and harmonic series. Topics surveyed include existence proofs, partitions, finite calculus, generating combinatorial objects, and algorithm analysis. Prerequisite: CALCULUS II [MATH 122]. [CMU course 21-301]

12.1.9. Linear Algebra [Math 341]

Description: Vector spaces, linear transformations, orthogonality and inner product spaces, projections, dual spaces, spectral theory for normal transformation, Jordan canonical form. Prerequisite: COMBINATORIAL ANALYSIS [MATH 301/CS251] [CMU course 21-341]

12.1.10. Numerical Methods [Math 369 / CS 352]

Description: Algorithmic oriented course in computer problem solving. The basic principles of numerical analysis are developed and used to solve problems involving networks and graphs, non-linear equations, differential equations, and data analysis. Prerequisite: METHODS OF APPLIED MATH I [MATH 259]. [CMU course 21-369]

12.1.11. Modern Algebra [Math 473 / CS 452]

Description: Spectral theorem, Jordan canonical form, groups, integral
domains, fields, polynomials, unique factorization domains, rings and
ideals, coding theory. Prerequisite: LINEAR ALGEBRA [MATH 341] [CMU
course 21-473]

12.1.12. Applied Graph Theory [Math 484 / CS 430]

Description: Basic terminology, cycles, trees, connectivity, planarity,
coloring, matching, graph algorithms, spanning trees, binary search trees.
Prerequisite: COMBINATORIAL ANALYSIS [MATH 301/CS 251] [CMU
course 21-484] *See description of* ADVANCED ALGORITHMS [430] *in
Section 11.3.10.*

12.1.13. Numerical Mathematics I and II [Math 704 and 705]

Description: Review of linear algebra, solution of partial differential
equations by finite element and finite difference methods, direct and
iterative methods, adaptive grid methods. Prerequisite: NUMERICAL
METHODS [MATH 369/CS352] [CMU course 21-704, 705]

12.1.14. Large-Scale Scientific Computing [Math 712 / CS 453]

Description: Review of scientific problems where computer modelling is
important, design of algorithms, supercomputer architectures, algorithms
for   parallel   computer   structures.   Prerequisite: NUMERICAL
MATHEMATICS II [MATH 705] or permission of instructor. [CMU course
21-712]

12.2. Statistics Courses

12.2.1. Probability and Applied Statistics for Physical Science and Engineering I [Stat 211 / CS 250]

Description: This course provides an introduction to probability for students
in engineering and science. The use of probability theory is illustrated
with examples drawn from these fields.   Topics include elementary
probability theory, conditional probability and independence, random
variables, distribution functions, joint and conditional distributions, law
of large numbers, and central limit theorem. Students desiring a more
mathematical treatment should register for 36-215. Prerequisite:
CALCULUS II [MATH 122] [CMU course 36-211]

12.2.2. Probability and Statistics I [Stat 215]

Description: An introductory probability course, designed for students whose interest is the theory of probability. Generally all mathematics majors should enroll in this course in their junior year. Provides the necessary background for study of mathematical statistics and further topics in probability theory. A good working knowledge of calculus is required. Use of the theory is illustrated with examples drawn from engineering, science, and management. Topics include elementary probability theory, combinatorial analysis, conditional probability, independence. random variables and distribution functions, conditional distributions, generating functions and moment generating functions, sampling distributions, law of large numbers, and central limit theorem. Prerequisite: CALCULUS II [MATH 122]. [CMU course 36-215]

12.2.3. Statistical Methods for Data Analysis I [Stat 219]

Description: This course presents basic concepts and operational methods of statistics for students in engineering, science and social science. Topics covered include reduction and summary of data, probability models and simulation, estimation, t-tests, goodness of fit tests, and multiple regression. The analysis of actual data sets is performed with Minitab, a statistical package requiring no previous computer experience. A section of this course will be offered for students with background and interests more oriented towards science, mathematics or engineering. No college-level prerequisites are necessary. [CMU course 36-219]

12.3. Electrical Engineering Courses

12.3.1. Linear Circuits: [EE 101 / CS 241]

Description: The objective of this course is to develop an understanding of the basic technical and mathematical skills required for the analysis of electrical systems. The concepts of charge, current, voltage, capacitance, inductance, energy and power are emphasized. Kirchoff's current and voltage laws, loop and node analyses, linear voltage current characteristics and superposition are introduced. The analytical and numerical solution of both difference and differential equations with constant coefficients and initial/boundary conditions, which arise in engineering problems is presented and used for the solution of first- and second-order differential equations which characterize R-C, R-L and R-L-C circuits. Consideration is given to the transient and sinusoidal steady-state analysis of linear circuits, including the use of phasor notation and complex algebra. Corequisite: PROGRAMMING AND PROBLEM SOLVING [110] [CMU course 18-101]

12.3.2. Electronic Circuits I [EE 102 / CS 242]

Description: The objective of this course is to provide the student with a
solid understanding of the application of the principles learned in 18-101,
and to increase the student's abilities to perform engineering analysis and
synthesis. Semiconductor physics; operation of circuit devices; large and
small signal models; biasing and temperature stability; diode and
transistor circuits; feedback. Prerequisites: LINEAR CIRCUITS [EE 101],
METHODS OF APPLIED MATH I [MATH 259], PHYSICS II; ELECTRICITY AND
MAGNETISM [PHYSICS 123] [CMU course 18-102]

12.3.3. Introduction to Digital Systems [EE 133]

Description: Description of fundamental digital devices; basic switching
circuit theory and design, including combinational and sequential logic
circuits; finite state machines; register transfer level logic design,
including modular components and their interconnection into data
processing units; simple processor architecture. Corequisite:
PROGRAMMING AND PROBLEM SOLVING [110] [CMU course 18-133]
Note: This course is very similar to CS course 240 as defined in this report.

12.3.4. Linear Systems Analysis [EE 218]

Description: This course presents a unified analytic treatment of continuous
time and discrete-time linear systems theory, and is intended to develop
facility in the mathematical characterization of these systems and their
performance in the time and frequency domains. Topics include
convolution, Fourier series and transforms, sampling theorems, LaPlace
transforms, Z-transforms, and applications of these methods to problems
in control and communications. Prerequisite: ELECTRONIC CIRCUITS I
[EE 102/CS 242]. [CMU course 18-218]

12.3.5. Electronic Circuits II [EE 221 / CS 340]

Description: Continuation of analog circuit analysis: feedback amplifiers;
frequency response; stability; operational amplifiers; op-amp
characterstics; op-amp circuits; waveform generators; oscillators; tuned
circuits, power amplifiers; amplifier classification; harmonic distortion.
Prerequisite: ELECTRONIC CIRCUITS I [EE 102/CS 242] [CMU course
18-221]

12.3.6. Analysis and Design of Digital Circuits [EE 222 / CS 341]

Description: This course introduces some advanced topics in the design and
analysis of digital circuits. Topics to be discussed include the analysis of
RTL, DTL, TTL, and ECL gates plus MIS components such as an ALU
and lookahead carry adder with emphasis on performance limitations

(noise margins, propagation delay, fan-in, fan-out, etc.); analysis of noise, cross-talk and reflections in IC interconnections; non-linear circuit analysis techniques including Newton-Raphson, Euler integration and Predictor-Corrector Methods; semiconductor processing for simple bipolar and metal-oxide devices along with the models developed in the course Prerequisite ELECTRONIC CIRCUITS II [EE 221/CS 340]. [CMU course 18-222]

12.3.7. Introduction to Solid State Electronics [EE 236]

Description: This course will introduce students to semiconductor solid state devices. The course will first cover the essential physics of semiconductor device operation, including the concepts of energy bands, the Fermi distribution function, transport of current by electrons and holes, tunneling, effective mass, etc. Following this, the operation of p-n junctions, Schottky barrier diodes, bipolar transistors, junction field effect transistors (JFET), and metal-oxide-semiconductor field effect transistors (MOSFET) will be discussed along with their use in integrated circuits. The course is intended for students with no prior experience or knowledge of semiconductors. Sophomores and higher level students who have completed Physics III, Electricity and Magnetism, are all well qualified to take this course. Prerequisite: PHYSICS III: ELECTRICITY AND MAGNETISM [PHYSICS 123] or permission of instructor. [CMU course 18-236]

12.3.8. Introduction to Computer Architecture [EE 247 / CS 440]

An outline for this course is given in Section 11.3.10.

12.3.9. Fundamentals of Control [EE 301]

Description: An introduction to the fundamental principles and main ideas of classical feedback control and its application. Emphasis is on problem formulation and the analysis and synthesis of servo-mechanisms using frequency domain techniques. Topics include analytical; graphical, analog techniques for treating automatic control systems; analysis of performance, stability criteria, realizability, and speed of response; compensation methods in the frequency domain, root-locus design, and pole-zero synthesis techniques; the use of analog computers in control systems; systems with delay and computer control systems; state-space description of linear systems; and non-linearities in control systems. Prerequisite: LINEAR SYSTEMS ANALYSIS [EE 218]. [CMU course 18-301]

12.4. Psychology Courses

12.4.1. Psychology of Learning and Problem Solving [Psy 113]

Description: A course aimed at increasing students' learning and problem-solving skills through understanding and applying topics in cognitive psychology. Topics covered will include representing problems searching for solutions, making decisions, learning and creativity. Emphasis will be placed on the acquisition of skills which can be transferred to the student's own area of interest. [CMU course 85-113]

12.4.2. Information Processing Psychology and Artificial Intelligence [Psy 213]

Description: Analysis of computer programs for producing intelligent behavior and their relationship to human information processing. The course focuses on perceptual information processing, memory systems, problem-solving and language processing. Students will write programs to simulate aspects of human information processing. rerequisites: Ability to program in some computer language. [CMU course 85-213]

12.4.3. Human Factors [Psy 363]

Description: The purpose of the course is to acquaint students with a rapidly expanding area of psychology, investigating the effects of human factors on cognitive and behavioral functioning. Central to the area is the notion that physical and social environments should be planned and constructed in a way that maximizes the fit between those environments and the psychological characteristics of the people that will inhabit them. In general, the course will focus on the use of machines as aides to human functioning. Included will be a discussion of the role that computers can play in information processing and human problem solving. Prerequisites: any 100- or 200-level psychology course. [CMU course 85-363]

12.4.4. Cognitive Processes and Problem Solving [Psy 411]

Description: Psychological processes in thinking and problem solving; relation of language to thinking; relation of perception and imagery to problem solving; semantics and internal representations; development of information processing capacity. Methods for studying thinking empirically; constructing and testing computer simulation models of adult's and children's thinking. Prerequisite: consent of the instructor. [CMU course 85-411]

12.4.5. Thinking [Psy 417]

Description: The course is intended as an extension of Psychology 411. It will review research on higher-level mental processes and the implications of this research. Possible topics include knowledge representation, pattern recognition, symbolic knowledge, schematic knowledge, memory for facts, skill acquisition, problem-solving, reasoning, language comprehension, language generation, and language acquisition. The factual content will mainly come from assigned readings and class discussions. Also, students will be required to perform a series of projects simulating various cognitive processes. Grade will be based on these simulation assignments and a final take-home. Prerequisite: Instructor's permission. [CMU course 85-417]

12.5. Engineering and Public Policy Courses

12.5.1. Law and Technology [EPP 321]

Description: The interaction of law and technology is considered in several areas: the environment, safety and health, product liability and patents and trade secrets. The public policy which emerges as law in these areas arises from forums such as public hearings or courts of law. The focus of the course is twofold: (1) understanding present law in these areas, and (2) using the data from prior public hearings in at least two of these areas to evaluate critically the nature and validity of the technological input used in reaching the public policy decision. Prerequisite: A course in basic legal concepts and practice. [CMU course 19-321]

12.5.2. Telecommunications Policy Analysis [EPP 402]

Description: This course reviews the physical principles and capabilities of modern telecommunications systems and surveys state-of-the art technology. Economic, cultural, political, and health-related impacts of telecommunications are discussed. The concept of the electromagnetic spectrum as a scarce but nondepletable resource and questions of economic efficiency and distributional equity will be considered as bases for national and international regulation. Cost-risk benefit determination and allocation will be studied using case studies (e.g.,telephone rate design, direct broadcast satellite licensing, ELF submarine communications alternatives). Prerequisites: PRINCIPLES OF ECONOMICS [ECON 100], junior standing. [CMU course 19-402/18-402]

12.5.3. Policy Issues in Computing [EPP 380 / CS 380]

As computers and automation become more pervasive, it becomes the responsibility of those who understand this technology to be aware of its effects on society and to be able to interpret it to both laymen and policy makers. This course is intended for students with expertise in computer science, and it will address the effects of specific computer technologies such as networks, very large databases, and robot automation. Prerequisites: FUNDAMENTAL STRUCTURES OF COMPUTER SCIENCE I AND II [211/212] plus any 300-level computer science course.

12.6. Engineering Courses

12.6.1. Real Time Computing in the Laboratory [Engr 252]

Description: The goal of this course is to introduce students to the use of dedicated microcomputers in laboratory situations, by covering those basics in computer organization and pertinent software concepts not taught in PROGRAMMING AND PROBLEM SOLVING [110]. It will require laboratory work, and will draw data gathering and real-time control examples and applications from various engineering disciplines. Prerequisite: PROGRAMMING AND PROBLEM SOLVING [110]. [CMU course 39-252]

12.6.2. Analysis, Synthesis and Evaluation [Engr 300]

Description: Analysis, synthesis, and evaluation in the context of realistic engineering situations. The student learns through practice to deal with problems which require the use of skills that include modelling, analyses that range from mathematical to heuristic, the use of experimental methods, inventing, making judgments of value and need, and the making of decisions and recommendations. Problems are chosen to reflect interdisciplinary nature of engineering problems. Prerequisite: junior standing. [CMU course 39-300]

12.6.3. The History and Formulation of Research and Development Policy [Engr 401]

Description: This interdisciplinary course will study the modes of research and development over the course of the 20th century. It will examine the relationship between the institutions responsible for R&D, such as industry, government, universities and foundations, and how R&D has affected the course of technological change. The course will consider the goals of R&D policy and the factors that have gone into policy formulation. The last section of the course will deal with the future directions of R&D policy. [CMU course 39-401, 79-509]

12.6.4. Cost-Benefit Analysis [Engr 404]

Description: The course will be directed primarily to Engineering students. Approximately equal time will be devoted to theory and practical applications. Topics will include the concepts of costs and benefits, market valuation and the meaning of prices (explicit and imputed), efficiency, the distribution of wealth, effects of alternative property rights structures, externality, investment criteria, uncertainty and risk. Examples of cost-benefit analysis will be presented and techniques of estimating costs and benefits will be discussed. Finally students will be given the opportunity to improve their skills in evaluating projects and examining appropriate alternatives by means of a practical exercise. Prerequisite: PRINCIPLES OF ECONOMICS [ECON 100] OR DESIGN PROJECT [ENGR 300] [CMU course 39-404]

References

1. ACM Curriculum Committee on Computer Science. "Curriculum 68: Recommendations for Academic Programs in Computer Science." *Communications of the ACM 11*, 3 (March 1968), 151-197.

2. ACM Curriculum Committee on Computer Science. "Curriculum Recommendations for the Undergraduate Program in Computer Science." *SIGCSE Bulletin (ACM) 9*, 2 (June 1977), 1-16.

3. ACM Curriculum Committee on Computer Science. "Curriculum '78: Recommendations for the Undergraduate Program in Computer Science." *Communications of the ACM 22*, 3 (March 1979), 147-166.

4. Alfred V. Aho, John E. Hopcroft, and Jeffrey D. Ullman. *The Design and Analysis of Computer Algorithms.* Addison-Wesley, 1974.

5. Alfred V. Aho and Jeffrey D. Ullman. *Principles of Compiler Design.* Addison-Wesley, 1977.

6. Alfred V. Aho, John E. Hopcroft, and Jeffrey D. Ullman. *Data Structures and Algorithms.* Addison-Wesley, 1983.

7. D. Ballard and C. Brown. *Computer Vision.* Prentice-Hall, 1982.

8. C. Gordon Bell, J. Craig Mudge and John E. McNamara. *Computer Engineering: A DEC View of Hardware Systems Design.* Digital Press, 1978.

9. M. Ben-Ari. *Principles of Concurrent Programming.* Prentice-Hall, 1982.

10. Jon Louis Bentley. *Writing Efficient Programs.* Prentice-Hall, Inc., 1982.

11. Jon Louis Bentley. "Programming Pearls." *Communications of the ACM 26*, 8 (August 1983). Regular column.

12. Garrett Birkhoff and Thomas C. Bartee. *Modern Applied Algebra.* McGraw-Hill, 1970.

13. Barry W. Boehm. *Software Engineering Economics.* Prentice-Hall, Inc, 1981.

14. J. A. Bondy and U. S. R. Murty. *Graph Theory with Applications.* American Elsevier, 1976.

15. G.S. Boolos and R.C. Jeffrey. *Computability and Logic.* Cambridge University Press, 1974.

16. Brady et al. (eds). *Robot Motion.* MIT Press, 1982.

17. Frederick P. Brooks, Jr.. *The Mythical Man-month: Essays on Software Engineering.* Addison-Wesley, 1975.

18. Marc H. Brown, Norman Meyrowitz, and Andries van Dam. Personal Computers Networks and Graphical Animation: Rationale and Practice for Education. ACM SIGCSE 14th Annual Technical Symposium, Association for Computing Machinery, February, 1983.

19. E. Charniak, C.K. Riesbeck, and D.V. McDermott. *Artificial Intelligence Programming.* Lawrence Erlbaum Associates, Hillsdale, New Jersey, 1980.

20. Michale J. Clancy and Donald E. Knuth. A Programming and Problem-Solving Seminar. Tech. Rept. Technical Report Stan-CS-77-606, Stanford University, April, 1977.

21. CMU Graduate School of Industrial Administration. Announcements for 1954-1956. CMU Catalog, 1954.

22. Carnegie-Mellon University. Carnegie-Mellon University Undergraduate Catalogue 1981-1983. CMU Catalog, 1981.

23. W. Corwin and W. Wulf. SL230 - A Software Laboratory Intermediate Report. Carnegie-Mellon University Computer Science Department, May, 1972.

24. Bruce W. Arden (ed.). *What Can Be Automated? The Computer Science and Engineering Research Study (COSERS).* MIT Press, 1981.

25. Committee on the Undergraduate Program in Mathematics. A General Curriculum in Mathematics for Colleges. Rep. to Math. Assoc. of America, CUPM, 1965.

26. N.J. Cutland. *Computability: An Introduction to Recursive Function Theory.* Cambridge University Press, 1980.

27. O.J. Dahl, E.W. Dijkstra, and C.A.R. Hoare. *Structured Programming.* Academic Press, 1982.

28. C.J. Date. *The System Programming Series: An Introduction to Database Systems Volume 1.* Addison-Wesley, Reading, MA, 1981.

29. C.J. Date. *The System Programming Series: An Introduction to Database Systems Volume 2.* Addison-Wesley, Reading, MA, 1983.

30. E.W. Dijkstra. Co-operating Sequential Processes. In F. Genuys, Ed., *Programming Languages*, Academic Press, 1968, pp. 43-112.

31. Edsger W. Dijkstra. *A Discipline of Programming.* Prentice-Hall, Inc., 1976.

32. Robert E. Doherty. The Development of Professional Education. CMU, Carnegie Press, 1950.

33. R.G. Dromey. *How to Solve it by Computer.* Prentice-Hall, 1982.

34. H. Enderton. *A Mathematical Introduction to Logic.* Academic Press, 1972.

35. Alan Feuer and Narain Gehani (editors). *Comparing and Assessing Programming Languages.* Prentice-Hall, 1984.

36. Lawrence Flon, Paul N. Hilfinger, Mary Shaw and Wm. A. Wulf. A Fundamental Computer Science Course that Unifies Theory and Practice. Proceedings of the SIGCSE/CSA Technical Symposium of Computer Science Education, February, 1978, pp. 255-259.

37. J.D. Foley and A. Van Dam. *Fundamentals of Interactive Computer Graphics.* Addison-Wesley, 1982.

38. Michael R. Garey and David S. Johnson. *Computers and Intractability: A Guide to the Theory of NP-Completeness.* W. H. Freeman and Company, 1979.

39. David B. Garlan and Philip L. Miller. GNOME: An Introductory Programming Environment Based on a Family of Structure Editors. Proceedings of the ACM SIGSOFT/SIGPLAN Software Engineering Symposium on Practical Software Development Environments, ACM, May, 1984, pp. 65-72.

40. Judith L. Gersting. *Mathematical Structures for Computer Science.* W.H. Freeman, 1982.

41. M.J.C. Gordon. *The Denotational Description of Programming Languages.* Springer-Verlag, 1979.

42. Paul E. Green, Jr. The Structure of Computer Networks. In *Computer Network Architectures and Protocols*, Paul E. Green, Jr., Ed.,Plenum Press, 1982, ch. 1, pp. 3-31.

43. David Gries. *Compiler Construction for Digital Computers.* Wiley, 1971.

44. David Gries. *The Science of Programming.* Springer-Verlag, 1981.

45. Ralph E. Griswold and Madge T. Griswold. *A SNOBOL4 Primer.* Prentice-Hall, Inc, 1973.

46. A.N. Habermann. *Introduction to Operating System Design.* Science Research Associates, Inc., 1976.

47. Frank Harary. *Graph Theory.* Addison-Wesley, 1969.

48. John R. Hayes. *The Complete Problem Solver.* Franklin Institute Press, 1981.

49. Peter Hibbard, Andy Hisgen, Jonathan Rosenberg, Mary Shaw, and Mark Sherman. *Studies in Ada Style.* Springer-Verlag, 1981.

50. Paul N. Hilfinger, Mary Shaw, Wm. A. Wulf and Lawrence Flon. Introducing "Theory" in the Second Programming Course. Proceedings of the Ninth SIGCSE Technical Symposium, August, 1978.

51. C.A.R. Hoare. "Communicating Sequential Processes." *Communications of the ACM 21*, 8 (August 1978), 666-677.

52. R.C. Holt, E.D. Lazowska, G.S. Graham and M.A. Scott. *Structured Concurrent Programming with Operating Systems Applications.* Addison-Wesley, 1978.

53. J.E. Hopcroft and J.D. Ullman. *Introduction to Automata Theory Languages and Computation.* Addison-Wesley, 1979.

54. Education Committee (Model Curriculum Subcommittee) of the IEEE Computer Society. A Curriculum in Computer Science and Engineering. IEEE Computer Society, November, 1976. Committee Report.

55. The Model Program Committee, Educational Activities Board. The 1983 IEEE Computer Society Model Program in Computer Science and Engineering. IEEE Computer Society, December, 1983.

56. ITT Programming. *Proceedings of the Workshop on Reusability in Programming.* Workshop on Reusability in Programming, Stratford, Connecticut, Stratford, Connecticut, 1983.

57. Johnsonbaugh, Richard. *Discrete Mathematics.* Macmillan, 1984.

58. Elaine Kant. "A Semester Course in Software Engineering." *Software Engineering Notes 6*, 4 (August 1981), 52-76.

59. B.W. Kernighan and P.J. Plauger. *Software Tools in Pascal.* Addison-Wesley, 1981.

60. Donald E. Knuth. *The Art of Computer Programming.* Volume 1: *Fundamental Algorithms.* Addison-Wesley, 1973.

61. Donald E. Knuth. *The Art of Computer Programming.* Volume 3: *Sorting and Searching.* Addison-Wesley, 1973.

62. Donald E. Knuth. "Computer Science and Its Relation to Mathematics." *American Mathematical Monthly 81*, 4 (April 1974).

63. Donald E. Knuth and Allan A. Miller. A Programming and Problem-Solving Seminar. Tech. Rept. Technical Report Stan-CS-81-863, Stanford University, June, 1981.

64. Donald E. Knuth. *The Art of Computer Programming.* Volume 2: *Seminumerical Algorithms.* Addison-Wesley, 1981.

65. Imre Lakatos. *Proofs and Refutations: The Logic of Mathematical Discovery.* Cambridge University Press, 1976.

66. Butler W. Lampson. "Hints for Computer System Design." *IEEE Software 1*, 1 (January 1984), 11-28.

67. Eugene L. Lawler. *Combinatorial Optimization: Networks and Matroids.* Holt, Rinehart, and Winston, 1976.

68. Henry Ledgard and Michael Marcotty. *The Programming Languge Landscape.* Science Research Associates, 1981.

69. Letters to the editor. "Comments on the Mathematical Content of Curriculum '78." *Communications of the ACM 23*, 6 (June 1980), 356-359.

70. H.R. Lewis and C.H. Papadimitriou. *Elements of the Theory of Computation.* Prentice-Hall, 1981.

71. C.L. Liu. *Introduction to Combinatorial Mathematics.* McGraw-Hill, 1968.

72. C.L. Liu. *Elements of Discrete Mathematics.* McGraw-Hill, 1977.

73. Jack Lochhead. The Mathematical Needs of Students in the Physical Sciences. In *The Future of College Mathematics*, Anthony Ralston and Gail Young, Eds., Springer-Verlag, 1983, pp. 55-70.

74. Bruce J. MacLennan. *Principles of Programming Languages: Design, Evaluation, and Implementation.* Holt, Rinehart, Winston, 1969.

75. Zohar Manna. *Mathematical Theory of Computation.* McGraw-Hill, 1974.

76. Manna, Zohar and Waldinger, Richard. Structured Programming with Recursion. Tech. Rept. STAN-CS-77-640, Stanford Artificial Intelligence Laboratory, January, 1978.

77. Carver Mead and Lynn Conway. *Introduction to VLSI Systems.* Addison-Wesley, 1980.

78. Milner, R.. *A Calculus of Communicating Systems.* Springer Verlag, 1980.

79. Marvin Minsky. *Computation: Finite and Infinite Machines.* Prentice-Hall, 1967.

80. Glenford J. Myers. *Software Reliability Principles and Practices.* Wiley Interscience, 1976.

81. Glenford J. Myers. *Composite/Structured Design.* Van Nostrand Reinhold, 1978.

82. William M. Newman and Robert F. Sproull. *Principles of Interactive Computer Graphics.* McGraw-Hill, 1979.

83. J.E. Nicholls. *The Structure and Design of Programming Languages.* Addison-Wesley, 1975.

84. N.J. Nilsson. *Principles of Artificial Intelligence.* Tioga Press, Palo Alto, CA, 1980.

85. National Science Foundation and the Department of Education. Science and Engineering: Education for the 1980's and Beyond. U.S. Government Printing Office, Washington, D.C., 1980.

86. Sandra Pakin. *APL\360 Reference Manual, Second Edition.* Science Research Associates, Inc., 1972.

87. Christos H. Papadimitriou and K. Steiglitz. *Combinatorial Optimization: Algorithms and Complexity.* Prentice-Hall, 1982.

88. F.W. Paul, D.L. Feucht, B.R. Teare, Jr., C.P. Neuman and D.Tuma. Analysis, Synthesis and Evaluation—Adventures in Professional Engineering Problem Solving. Proc. Fifth Annual Frontiers in Education Conference, IEEE and the Amer. Soc. for Engr. Ed., October, 1975, pp. 244-251.

89. R. Paul. *Robot Manipulators: Mathematics, Programming, and Control.* MIT Press, 1981.

90. Pierce, J. R. and Posner, E. C.. *Introduction to Communication Science and Systems.* Plenum Press, 1980.

91. George Polya. *Mathematical Discovery.* John Wiley and Sons, 1962.

92. George Polya. *How to Solve It.* Princeton University Press, 1973.

93. Terrence W. Pratt. *Programming Languages: Design and Implementation (second edition).* Prentice-Hall, Inc., 1984.

94. Anthony Ralston and Mary Shaw. "Curriculum '78—Is Computer Science Really that Unmathematical?" *Communications of the ACM 23*, 2 (February 1980), 67-70.

95. Anthony Ralston. "Computer Science, Mathematics, and the Undergraduate Curricula in Both." *American Mathematical Monthly 88*, 7 (1981).

96. Edward M. Reingold, Jurg Nievergelt, and Narsingh Deo. *Combinatorial Algorithms: Theory and Practice.* Prentice-Hall, 1977.

97. Elaine Rich. *Artificial Intelligence.* McGraw-Hill, 1983.

98. H. Rogers. *Theory of Recursive Functions and Effective Computability.* McGraw-Hill, 1967.

99. Moshe F. Rubinstein. *Patterns of Problem Solving.* Prentice-Hall, Inc., 1975.

100. Roger C. Schank and Christopher K. Riesbeck. *Inside Computer Understanding.* Lawrence Erlbaum Associates, 1981.

101. W.L. Scherlis and M.Shaw. Mathematics Curriculum and the Needs of Computer Science. In *The Future of College Mathematics*, Anthony Ralston and Gail Young, Eds., Springer-Verlag, 1983, pp. 89-97.

102. Robert Sedgewick. *Algorithms.* Addison-Wesley, 1983.

103. Mary Shaw. Working Papers on an Undergraduate Computer Science Curriculum. Tech. Rept. CMU-CS-83-101, Carnegie-Mellon University, Computer Science Department, February, 1983.

104. Mary Shaw, Stephen Brookes, Bill Scherlis, Alfred Spector, and Guy Steele. Plan for Developing an Undergraduate Computer Science Curriculum. CMU CS Curriculum Design Note 82-02, 1982.

105. Martin Shooman. *Software Engineering.* McGraw-Hill, 1983.

106. Daniel P. Siewiorek, C. Gordon Bell, and Allen Newell. *Computer Structures: Principles and Examples.* McGraw-Hill, 1982.

107. D.F. Stanat and D.F. McAlister. *Discrete Mathematics in Computer Science.* Prentice-Hall, Inc., 1977.

108. Lynn Arthur Steen. Developing Mathematical Maturity. In *The Future of College Mathematics*, Anthony Ralston and Gail Young, Eds., Springer-Verlag, 1983, pp. 99-110.

109. H.S. Stone. *Discrete Mathematical Structures and Their Applications.* Science Research Associates, Inc., 1973.

110. Joseph E. Stoy. *Denotational Semantics: The Scott-Strachey Approach To Programming Language Theory.* MIT Press, 1977.

111. Andrew S. Tanenbaum. *Computer Networks.* Prentice-Hall, Engelwood Cliffs, NJ, 1981.

112. Tim Teitelbaum, Thomas Reps, Susan Horwitz. The Why and Wherefore of the Cornell Program Synthesizer. Proceedings of the ACM SIGPLAN SIGOA Symposium on Text Manipulation, Cornell University, June, 1981, pp. 8-16.

113. R.D. Tennent. *Principles of Programming Languages.* Prentice-Hall, 1981.

114. J.P. Tremblay and R.P. Manohar. *Discrete Mathematical Structures With Applications to Computer Science.* McGraw-Hill, 1975.

115. D.T. Tuma and F. Reif. *Problem Solving and Education: Issues in Teaching and Research.* Lawrence Erlbaum Associates, 1980.

116. Jeffrey D. Ullman. *Principles of Database Systems.* Computer Science Press, 1982.

117. Jeffrey D. Ullman. *Computational Aspects of VLSI.* Computer Science Press, 1984.

118. The CSD Undergraduate Program Committee. Initial Report on an Undergraduate CS Program. CMU internal memorandum, 1980.

119. Chris Van Wyk and Donald E. Knuth. A Programming and Problem-Solving Seminar. Tech. Rept. Technical Report Stan-CS-79-707, Stanford University, January, 1979.

120. D. vanDalen. *Logic and Structure.* Springer-Verlag, 1980.

121. Richard L. Wexelblat, editor. *History of Programming Languages.* Academic Press, 1981.

122. Wayne A. Wickelgren. *How to Solve Problems.* W.H. Freeman and Company, 1974.

123. Patrick Henry Winston and Berthold Klaus Paul Horn. *LISP.* Addison-Wesley, Reading, Mass, 1981.

124. P.H. Winston. *Artificial Intelligence.* Addison-Wesley, Reading, MA, 1984. Second edition.

125. Niklaus Wirth. *Algorithms + Data Structures = Programs.* Prentice-Hall, 1976.

126. William Wulf, Richard K. Johnsson, Charles B. Weinstock, Steven O. Hobbs, and Charles M. Geschke. *The Design of an Optimizing Compiler.* American Elsevier Publishing Co., 1975.

127. William A. Wulf, Mary Shaw, Paul N. Hilfinger, and Lawrence Flon. *Fundamental Structures of Computer Science.* Addison-Wesley, 1981.

128. Edward Yourdon and Larry L. Constantine. *Structured Design Fundamentals of a Discipline of Computer Program and Systems Design.* Prentice-Hall, 1979.

129. Marvin V. Zelkowitz, and Alan C. Shaw, and John D. Gannon. *Principles of Software Engineering and Design.* Prentice-Hall, 1979.

Index